The Waterworks

Tips, Inspiration, and Advice for Watercolor Artists

Ken Austin, NWS

Copyright © 2018 Ken Austin

All rights reserved.

ISBN:
ISBN-13: 978-1718658400
ISBN-10: 1718658400

Except for use in a review, the reproduction or utilization of this work in any form or by any electronic, mechanical, or other means, now known or hereafter invented, including xerography, photocopying, and recording, and in any information storage and retrieval system is forbidden without the written permission of author or publisher.

Cover design by Jennifer Newcomb-Marine.
Book design by Elizabeth King Gerlach.
Author photo by Jane Austin.
Special thanks to Jeff Strong.

All paintings including cover "Red Boat, Green Boat" and back cover "Twitter Nacht Web", by Ken Austin.
www.kenaustinartist.com

1. Watercolor 2. Art 3. Painting

Published by Four Leaf Press
www.fourleafpress.com

Printing History: First Edition: May 2018
Printed in the United States of America.

For Jane

CONTENTS

	Introduction	9
1	Inspirations	11
2	Style and Technique	35
3	Learning Curves	59
4	Masters Class	85
5	Choice Points	101
6	Showtime	117
7	Colormaking	141
8	Perspectives on Painting & Composition	157
9	Community Chest	175
10	Keep an Open Mind	201

Thanks and Dedications

This book is dedicated to the members of the Central Florida Watercolor Society based in Orlando, Florida. I started this organization in 1996 and in 1997 it was officially founded as a 501c-3 organization. They are a great group and will continue to be.

I also dedicate this book to those who, through their perseverance, patience and outspokenness, gave me the assurance to write, edit and publish it. Those I wish to thank most are:

F. Jane Austin (editing and advice) an excellent writer herself.

And for all the hard work and constant support she's given as editor, organizer, proofer, advisor and publishing consultant, and pushing me forward, my dear daughter, a published award-winning author; Elizabeth King Gerlach.

In addition, I want to thank those great teachers who have encouraged, discouraged and outraged me over the last 25 or so years; but who also taught me almost all of what I now know about watercolor:
Bob Davis, Polly Hammet, Skip Lawrence, Carl Molno, Virginia Cobb, Carol Barnes, and Pat San Soucie.

And countless others from my mother, Betty H. Austin, (a terrific Alabama artist) to my grandkids for their great flights of fancy in art.

Many, many thanks to all! I owe you big time.

Introduction

For almost 20 years I've written regular articles for our local watercolor society's newsletter and those writings have become this book. Publication, of course, is a team effort. These considerations require lots of rewriting, re-editing, design, and the help of others, all of which have gone into making this (I hope) a readable, user-friendly book. While I'm not a writer by trade (I spent over 60 years as a student/architect/city planner/artist), I do enjoy sharing my insights with others, insights gained by a virtual lifetime of familiarity with watercolor. My mother, a talented, well-educated artist, would take me with her on her plein air safaris when I was four years old. She'd say, "Paint me a picture!"- and I would. In fact, I continued painting with her occasionally until I was a teenager. As a result, I've had a lifelong love of watercolor and art.

Through time, learning about art in its broader sense has changed and improved my own art. That change in understanding is the source of this writing. This book isn't so much about the nuts and bolts of watercolor painting (even though a few show through), but mostly about my relationship with watercolor art, its makers, its making, and the joy and suffering throughout the process of working in this beautiful medium. For me it has been, and I hope continues to be, both engaging and rewarding work.

I've had the great fortune to learn from terrific artists and art teachers; I've seen great works of art and architecture all over the U.S., Mexico and Europe and painted with friends and students who taught me more than I could have learned in any university. Most importantly, I've had more than my share of support and understanding from my family, which at times was about all the support I had.

In response to my fellow members of the Central Florida Watercolor Society who for years have urged me to publish these pieces, I hope they, especially, enjoy and profit from their re-readings. And, of course, I hope you, the reader, will too.

Ken Austin, NWS, FWS, FLAG

1
INSPIRATIONS

Big Influences

Who are your big influences in art? Did your mom tell you to stay inside the lines when you color? Did your high school teacher tell you it wasn't required? Was there a chance happening where you took a wrong turn and ended up in the parking lot of an art museum or gallery? Or do you have a teacher who guided and supported you through the tough spots and allowed you to develop in your own way?

We all are influenced by who raises us and how, those who teach us, and those whose work we admire or dislike. All are powerful influences, and on top of that we are powerful influences on ourselves. My influences were powerful too, beginning with my mom, a strong-willed woman who gained a Master's in art and taught art all her life. In architecture school I learned about art from friends and classmates in fine arts, through passionate discussions, arguments, and lots of beer. We in architecture had to learn how to draw and paint buildings, trees, bushes, lawns, roads, parking lots, skies, figures (very basic ones, of course), etc., and therefore had to learn those basics of color, drawing, perspective, and composition, with many a rule that we later found didn't apply.

I ended up a design architect half of my career, and so kept up with my drawing and rendering skills. I got to Houston, TX in 1975 and, about 1980, I decided I needed art lessons, so I took a class with Polly Hammett. Her classes seemed loose, but were packed with useful information. Polly and I ended up sharing a studio, where I learned even more just by observing and talking. To my amazement, my architectural designs improved immensely.

After moving to Orlando, FL in 1987 I found myself harkening back to things she professed, and moved toward teaching the way she did. We're still close, and keep in close touch. Her words and work are still in my mind as I paint today, as are those from others who've made a strong impression.

I believe it pays to think about the influences you've had in art. For one, you can compare what you do now to what you did before that influence, and by so doing, begin to analyze what you paint and why. If it's from someone who knew nothing about art (your favorite aunt said all art was stupid), maybe you don't need it. If it contrasts with your overall approach and direction, maybe you don't need it. If it's something once said to you in a workshop, and it helped you in that particular moment, maybe you should expand on it.

We all have our origins and destinations. I think we all go through a two-sided process of learning how to paint. One reflects what suits us and our pursuit toward a specific desired idea, the other beckons us to do what someone or something told us was the "only" or "right" way to succeed. Don't be afraid to throw out some things and incorporate new, better things. That's how we grow and succeed. And try to let only the positive things - those that make your work better - guide you in your quest for quality.

Looking For Inspiration

Carl Molno, that great, volatile watercolor artist and teacher from Brooklyn once laughed that as a student he and his classmates spent an entire Sunday driving all over the New England countryside, and went home with empty canvases because they "couldn't find anything worth painting." Carl then showed us his sketchbooks full of embryonic paintings, just waiting for a 20x30 sheet of Arches and a couple of hours for him to play midwife to his ideas. He did these sketches on coffee breaks at work, and in front of the TV, while riding in the car, etc.

He was teaching that inspiration does not come from the subject, but from within. <u>We</u> must find that subtle inner voice that says, "Get out and paint!" Well, maybe these ideas will help:

- Set yourself up a project so that you can paint a series of paintings regarding some central theme. It doesn't much matter what - put a red line around everything, or paint only the surrounding spaces, not the subjects, or paint everything in its opposite colors. As long as it's do-able, you'll find you are mesmerized by the new and different way of seeing/thinking.

- Change tools. Using a twig and ink to draw with can teach you more about character than all the books you can read.

- Take a course (portrait painting or figure study), in a new subject. Its challenges may make the old more interesting!

- Paint with a child. They have a completely different approach to art, and if you will learn, too, you may come out of it much the better artist.

- Form a painting group with new faces. Working with others is challenging, engaging, and educational. Not to mention <u>lots</u> of fun.

John Singer Sargent said, "I never paint *scenes*, I paint pictures!" He would walk out, randomly plant his easel, and produce a gorgeous painting. His wisdom was that the <u>scene</u> is not the art - the <u>painting</u> is the art. No matter what you have before you, *you* create the painting; and it's up to *you* to get inspired.

Flavors

I drove by a Baskin Robbins yesterday, and thought about the "31 Flavors". I don't know if they still have that many, but they were cuddled into a Dunkin Donuts, still selling lots of flavors, I bet. In some ways, I think art is like an ice cream store - or is it a box of chocolates, a la Forrest Gump? Nah, I like "flavors", because we think of paintings as being flavored - by color, history, style, subject, etc.

In fact, it might be a good exercise to look at your own work like historians and critics look at art. Think about where it came from; the look of it, the feel of it, the change from painting to painting, because we need to recognize what part is ours, what part is someone else's, how we feel about it, what are its roots, and how we've expressed those things on paper.

A good example might be one of my own paintings, "Geomancy I: Santa Fe", because it has several strong flavors in it, some mine, some others'. Before starting this painting, I'd decided to travel to New Mexico for a workshop with the great Virginia Cobb. Those visions of Taos and Santa Fe were floating in my head. I had just uncovered an old painting I did in a workshop with Pat San Soucie. The painting had its charms, but not enough to stand on its own, so it was never framed or hung. The way to improve it, I realized, was to make it another painting.

Pat lays down torn pieces of absorbent paper on a sheet of Arches, mixes watercolor into a liquid state, pours it into the torn paper and lifts the paper off when dry. This leaves color imprints of the paper and all its wet state curls and wrinkles. Color shapes on paper can make for a lively statement, but I had turned out a quiet, composed group of shapes that, to me, looked like geographic maps, or aerial photos. Since they were all irregular, it occurred to me that I could overpaint and complement these quiet geoforms with geometric, almost engineered shapes, giving an exciting contrast of layers, shapes and colors.

The painting took shape pretty quickly, with colors reminiscent of turquoise, coral, sunsets, and shapes like circles, straight lines, etc. These seemed to be highways and other engineering feats, while I emphasized some of the geomorphic shapes, giving over to river-like, lake-like land forms. After finishing, I darkened darks, made some cloud shapes, and stood back. I had painted a comment on nature tamed (or violated), specifically in that beautiful desert area. I was excited and felt good about knowing what I had said (though I don't think it was what I started out to say) and the way I said it. The flavor of the painting is clear. The geometry is attractive, but is unique. It doesn't observe or follow the lines of nature. The "natural" parts are similar, but are covered and cut by the "man-made" parts. We know what's on top of what.

I don't know where, exactly this all came from. But the flavors of some modern artists, Pat San Soucie of course, and those who geometrize nature (Cezanne? Wyeth?) and the contrast and conflict (Warhol? Kandinsky? Lichtenstein?) were all there for me to ponder. The colors were soft with accents, the flavors of Santa Fe - adobe homes with blue and orange trim, jewelry of colorful stones and silver - on and on. This was easy to know about, easy to answer. But maybe we should think on what we <u>don't</u> know about. Maybe then we learn more about ourselves and the art we make. By tasting the flavors.

It's Only Art!

So many of my students ask me, as they paint a simple exercise, "How can I make this look more like my subject?" It's a good question to ask, but not always simple to explain or even demonstrate. I usually try to show them where and how they can improve their work, but I find there are actually two sides to this issue.

One side says to reproduce on paper what you see in front of you. This is a common approach for artists, since it produces images of real things in real surroundings. We like doing this because it lets us reproduce the subject in watercolor, a medium that, because of its own character, can beautify the simplest scene.

The other side says that the artists are free to paint whatever and however they want, because it's a free country and artists are here to interpret, caricature, abstract or do whatever feels right. So who *is* right?

I don't know.

But I do know that the great art of our civilization is not art that copies nature to the gnat's hair, but art that pulls us into its subject. Regardless of whether that subject is a seascape, an abstract or a tomato soup can, the artists who created those great paintings had a big idea or a big feeling about what they wanted to communicate. No matter how unorthodox their methods, they got their ideas/feelings across to us, sometimes so profoundly, so intimately that we never forget them.

If a student's problem is in the drawing, or paint mixing, or application, I can help them with direction. But if the problem is in expression or messaging I can only offer suggestions or convey what the painting is saying to *me*. If it's not saying what the student/artist thinks it says, it might be failing. Of course, the problem may lie with the teacher (I was over 50 years old before I found the beauty in Henri Rousseau's strange paintings), so maybe more than one "expert" should critique the work.

But, for safety's sake, I'm offering a few ideas for you to consider as you work:

-If you have a clear goal, try to write it down in a simple phrase, and keep it in view.

-If you have trouble with materials, find solutions from other artists, books, online info, etc.

-If you're painting real things but they don't look right in proportion, direction or perspective, try some drawing classes or books or videos covering those specific issues, and practice, practice, practice.

-Try thinking of color and value in terms of the information they transmit to the viewer - which colors are "sad" or "happy", which are "strong" or "weak", etc.

-Keep the principles of design handy and use them to <u>critique</u> your work as it progresses – but don't let it <u>rule</u> your enjoyment of what you're doing.

-Keep the characteristics of colors in mind- how do you tone down a strong color or show two things of the same color in contrast? How do you arrange the colors to proceed or move through the painting? How do you pair up colors for best effect?

-Keep a piece of waste watercolor paper handy so you can see how your paints will look if you want to proceed with an idea but you're not sure of the outcome.

-Paint with friends who can give you help and for whom you can do the same.

-Finally: study art of all kinds and art history to gain insight and appreciation of the artists who created it. Much of it was a struggle for them, and their work can make yours easier.

   Keep your sense of humor handy. It will carry you through lots of bad washes, contest rejections, self-condemnation, confusion and, yes, heady success.

   It's been my opinion for many years that artists must find their own paths to creating works of beauty and meaning. Along the way we all need help and direction, some less than others, but few can find a way to success alone.

And a final word about it all, quoted from a noted local art expert: "Oh come on – IT'S ONLY ART!"

Playing Favorites

Do you have a favorite painter? I mean an artist whose work you admire beyond all others and, in at least some ways wish to imitate? Yes? Well, so do I. And so do most of us. And is it "correct" to do so? Sure. It is a free country, after all. We all love one or more "hero" artists and their art, and sometimes emulate them, either in our work or in some aspect of it.

I'm a fan of several famous artists, and while I don't think I've copied them, I've paid homage by using some little detail or flourish from them. I love Matisse's work, but my figure paintings are different; they are distorted, but not the sensuous ladies he presented. Much of my figure work is of female nudes who are ample in size with skin colored turquoise or lavender or red, but never flesh colored. Matisse's women were sometimes not natural colors either. He loved pattern and much of his work had a decorative feel to it. I like that too, and cover many of my paintings with pattern of my own design. Walls, rugs, floors, curtains, bedclothes, etc., it's all grist for my pattern mill. And I use the concepts freely, but without copying them, except for one thing that I lifted; I like to put a self-portrait on the wall, framed, of course, and/or another painting of the painting I'm painting. On the wall in the painting there's a picture of my painting. It's a pun, a joke and I love it. While it's not an original idea, it's a nod to the master.

The other great artist I admire is Paul Klee. A master of line and color, Klee had a prodigious output in his career, mostly of small, abstract pieces in ink, oils and watercolor. His work, while called modern, is to me, very dreamlike, as though he woke in the night and had to get his dream down on paper or canvas. Admired by many other modern artists of his day, he never succumbed to "isms"... Cubism, Constructivism, etc., but stuck to his own vision, a succinct, but often unknowable world of architectural and supernatural and known places and activities. While many of these had a sense of humor about them, some were more foreboding. I've never used any of his ideas or design approaches because I wouldn't know where to start. Nonetheless, I find myself thumbing through my books of his work, wishing I could paint like him.

Of course there are a bunch of artists whose work I really admire, and which informs me as to what art is really about. I could reel off a list of them here. But instead <u>you</u> need to think about whose work you admire and what you can learn from them. It may not be easy to learn from someone's work, when you won't have an opportunity to be with them and discuss it. So what do you do?

My approach is based on a couple of concepts to keep me from being a copyist (copying is a worthwhile way to learn an artist's technique, but should never be represented as one's own work).

1. Try to think about what it is that you like about the work and then, narrow down to one thing you can try e.g., is it the color? Is it the design? Is it because it

grabs you? Try to analyze the specifics of that one thing, and then try it in a painting of your own.

2. Don't try to <u>reproduce</u> the specific. If your efforts don't <u>look</u> like your hero's, but still make your painting better, you're way ahead. Try another. Do the same thing; keep working until you can use the same <u>concept</u> in your own work.

3. Strive to be original in how and what you paint - not just for originality's sake, but to give yourself some space to be creative. Try to understand your own creative process.

4. Learn the technique you need to provide the look you want. You can do it. I was painting a piece with some mackerel in it, and didn't know how to get the sheen and reflection on the scaly critters. So I sat down and worked it out by painting it over and over until I had it right. Simple? Yes, but we all want to just dive in like we had Walt Disney's magic brush. Ain't gonna happen.

5. Try to find classes or TV presentations or DVDs or any way you can to learn what the artist is/was trying to achieve, and what made her paint the way she did. If you know their goals you can often trace their trails toward achievement.

These are some quick ideas which, I admit, aren't

necessarily simple or easy to incorporate into your painting style or your educational approach, but they have worked for me.

Who Do You Paint For?

The question may seem strange, but a few days ago that particular question came to me, in a more personal, philosophical moment (and believe me, they are few), but I had to do some real self-examination to answer it. Now, my list of reasons are more than a handful, because I was raised by an artist, and was surrounded with art all my life, painted with watercolor most of my life, and have had lots of people tell me they like what I produce. Of course, lots of people *don't* like it and it *is* a free country after all (I hope, anyway) so I don't really need the support of everyone who walks into my studio...but I would be concerned if a majority *disliked* my work. So, after a brief discussion with our intelligent, talented editor, we decided I should explore this.

Do I paint to please my mom (many of us still act to please our parents, though they're long gone)? No, I never did after age 12. Do I paint to please a certain subset of artists? No, I don't care if they're realists, abstractionists, expressionists, pop, or whatever. While I appreciate compliments from artists whose work I admire, if they don't like my work, it's ok as long as I don't *have* to like theirs. But the fact is, I like most good art of any era, format or name, as long as I don't have to conform to anyone else's specific ideology of how and why I commit paint and time to a certain idea or feeling. Do I paint to be in shows and win awards? I used to, but now I usually just choose something I've already done, not especially for a submission.

So why bring it up?

Because many people choose a certain brand or "kind" of art or a particular artist's work to emulate/identify/partner with. Some do it on purpose, some because it's the way they were taught, some because they saw it in a magazine and have tried to work in that style and subject matter as a career. That's fine, but I believe in the efficacy of originality. We can all paint the same tree and everyone's painting will make the tree look different, regardless of how realistically it's presented.

My theory is (and it's not original) that we're all different and therefore we see or comprehend objects and ideas differently. Some of us paint circles and lines, some paint stories, some paint "real" things, some not so real, etc. - but are they painting as taught, or to sell, or as they see it all? Are they painting *things* or *relationships* between color, shape, line, size and direction? And WHO do they paint for?

I may not be the best example, but I try (try, try, try) to paint for myself with the potential viewer in mind. I try to make a painting that is interesting, involving and stated in my own manner. This doesn't make me a prize-winner or (unfortunately) a wealthy artist, but it keeps me on track for originality in my work. The artistry comes from study, invention and experience, all of which I've had aplenty.

An interesting example of how art can be the same yet different was apparent in the Orlando Museum of Art's show, "The Wyeths", featuring father, son and grandson of a family of artists, all famous in their own right, all considered "realists". In fact, the only thing "real" about their art was that they painted "real" things. N.C. Wyeth was a romantic, painting illustrations for stories of pirates, the American Revolution, and other action/historical scenes and landscapes. His son, Andrew, painted his Maine surroundings with landscapes, buildings, and people he knew and saw every day, but all composed in ways that made the paintings themselves abstract masterpieces. N.C.'s other children all were artists in their own way, all "realists", but all resolute in making art that was identifiably their own. Jamie, Andrew's son, was well known for realism, but his subjects seem more emotionally open, though often with a feeling of unrest.

I guess the point here is, there is no one way or one goal for artists. That's the reason you see differences between Winslow Homer and John Singer Sargent. They were watercolor realists, but the same subjects were day and night. They painted for *themselves*. They developed their own styles. They had their own ideas of what and how to paint. And they were outstanding artists who produced beautiful works, still enjoyed by millions of people a century later. So my idea is that learning technique doesn't make art. It's *what you do* with the technique, attitude, direction and knowledge that you have that makes art.

So, don't just paint like Homer. Make some of YOUR art! Paint for *yourself* and you'll be happy you did.

My Favorite Art Story

My mother was an exceptional artist with years of study at the Art Students' League in New York, a Master's degree in art, and a long teaching and painting history in Alabama and Mississippi.

Once, while working in Mississippi, a very conservative part of the country, she was changing studios and had hired a truck and driver to move her paintings. At that particular time she was deeply involved in figure painting and had done many nude studies in oil. Because there had been a light rain, all of these were neatly stacked uncovered, but with the painted (waterproof) sides up in the open-bed truck to protect them against dampness. As they headed for the new studio, my mom was close behind in her car when the truck went into a sharp curve in the road and spun out. No one was hurt, but the paintings had come loose and spilled out on the side of the road.

A young man immediately pulled out of the traffic to help. Assuring him that no one was injured, Mom asked him if he would help reload the paintings, since the skies were threatening again, and she was worried about rain. He quickly turned to and helped the hired man. As the loading finished, Mom asked if she could pay him something for his efforts. He said he would take the money, not for himself, but for his church. It turned out the Samaritan was a preacher in a conservative church with a small congregation. He and Mom exchanged thanks and he wished her well, got in his car and left.

It was only when she reached her new studio that my mom realized he had carefully loaded all the nude paintings face down.

Moral: No matter how much they respect you, or how nice they are, some people can't accept the work you do - it's ok.

My Second Most Favorite Art Story

My mother, the painter, was fully aware of her talents (which were significant), and when she was visiting us in Houston we would always visit the Museum of Fine Art, one of America's premiere general collections.

Once, as she was getting on in years, she asked me to go with her to the museum to meet with the Director. I asked what for, and she told me she had set up an appointment to ask for a retrospective exhibit of her work.

Now, as talented as she was, Mom's work was not up to that of Sargent, Homer, or a hundred other masters represented in the collection there. Nonetheless, chutzpah had carried her through on many occasions, and so I agreed to go with her.

We went the next day at the appointed time, and waited in the reception area until a door opened and a sociable, youngish man greeted us, smiling and shaking our hands. When we were all seated he asked her what he could do for her, whereupon on she promptly launched into her background, résumé, and a history of her achievements, all of which were true and remarkable in themselves, then said, "I want to know what I must do to have you mount a retrospective exhibit of my work?". Our host studied deeply for a moment, and then, with a regretful smile, said, "Well, Ms. Austin, I must tell you that our policy is to exhibit only works of artists who are no longer living." To which Mom replied, "Well, young man, I don't think it's worth that!"

Moral: We all have a limit to the price we'll pay for fame. Think about yours beforehand.

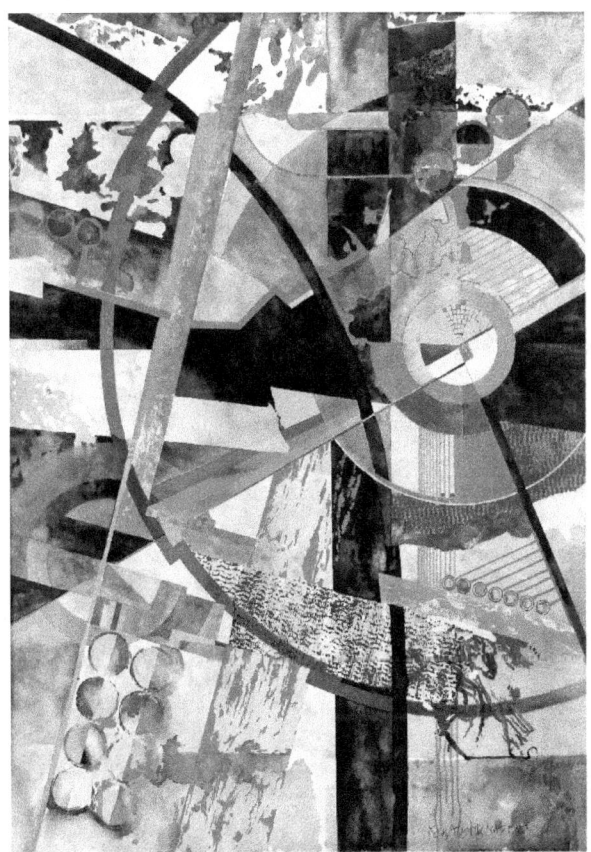

Geomancy III: I Believe

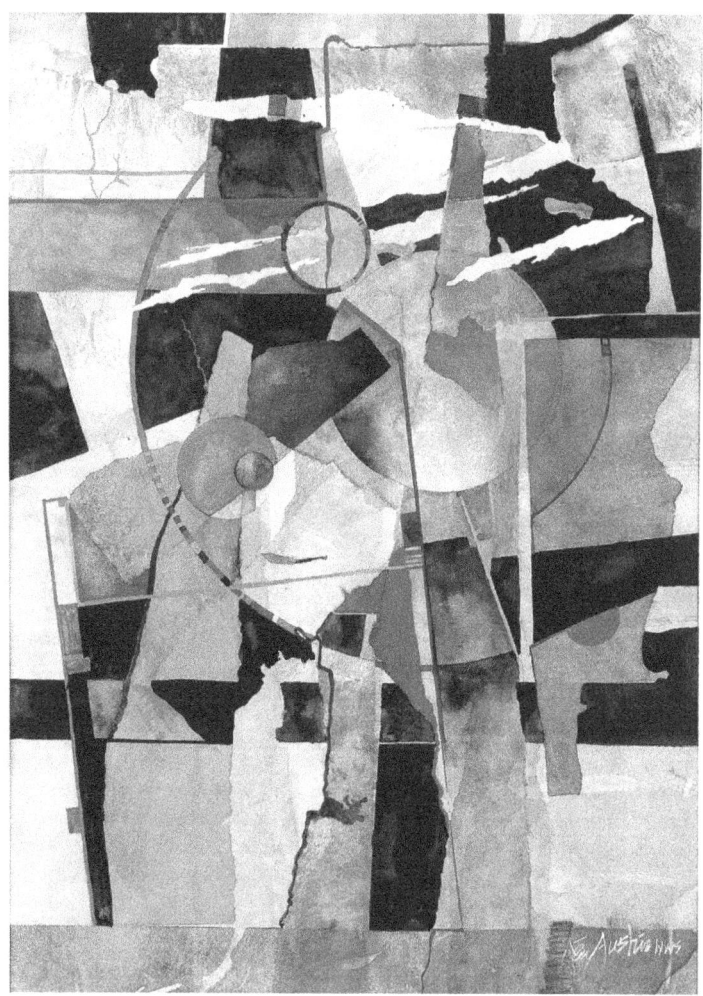

Geomancy I: Santa Fe

2
STYLE AND TECHNIQUE

How Do You Feel About That?

There are enough books on watercolor to fill more than one bookshelf in my house. They cover many aspects of painting in this medium, from which pigments to buy to how to make brush strokes appropriate for particular shapes. They speak of light and dark, complementary and analogous, weak and strong, shape and line, positive and negative, etc., etc., etc., but hardly ever do they use the word "feeling".

A few years back Alex Powers told me that he had, in the last few years, seen a great improvement in and mastery of design in the paintings he judged, but very little feeling. I didn't know exactly what he meant, but after a couple of sessions with Skip Lawrence I knew that I needed to make my paintings "feel" more. I'm still not sure I always get it right, but I do try to paint more meaningfully than I used to. Part of that is, I believe, because I'm a little more aware that it's important, and I do have some famous painters to thank for it.

"Well, what is it?" you say. "I have invested hundreds in paints, books, workshops, lessons, carved a studio out of spaces in my house, visited museums, lectures, etc., etc., etc. And you're telling me my work doesn't have *feeling*? Well, who cares?" You certainly have a fair argument against something as soft and fuzzy as "feeling", but the fact is, when you see a painting you love, even if you don't especially like the technique, the color, the composition or the other hundred technicalities that go into making a good painting, you know it must be the feeling. But a "what's left" definition isn't a good one. Let's try again.

I think paintings need a meaning. I think the meaning can be simple, "Beautiful scene", or, "Creepy tight spaces", or, more abstractly, any word that describes how we feel about something. How about, "Thinking", or, "Hot and humid", or "Cold"? Did you ever try to paint a word? Not just the letters, but how you respond when you hear it, consider it, "*feel* it", in other words. You might want to try this. Have a friend put together a list of 20 or 30 words that are evocative of feelings. Everything is allowable as long as it's not offensive, or simply something with little or no feelings attached to it. Then have a blind drawing for a word, and paint that word. How do you do that? If you draw a descriptive word like "shadow", what's going to give a shadow a feeling? Well, I'd start by expanding on "shadow"; daytime, nighttime? What causes one? What are the feelings I get from a shadow? How do I feel when I close my eyes and think, "shadow"? Which and what kind of feelings will I impart and how? Should color or value dominate? How will contrast affect the feeling? Should I paint a shadow?

See? There are lots of options. And words abound that can jumpstart a painting session; "pensive, rainfall, reflection, hot, jittery, calm, sweet, matching" and on and on. And it's great fun!

I'm starting to do this in my workshops, because I agree with Alex. We've become a big group of pretty picture artists. We know how to paint and what to paint, but we don't know the way to make them carry an emotional wallop. Or a little tinge of sadness. Or a little anxiety. Or a whole lot of contemplation. We artists are a special lot. We think we're better than the camera and the computer. We think *they* can't get nearly the emotional charge that an old-fashion hand-made watercolor can. But they can. I know because for my holiday E-cards I usually put one of my landscape paintings into Photoshop and change it into a scene that says "home for the holidays", Florida style. These always bring a big positive response, way more for the cards than the originals. Why?

Well, of course the December holidays and others bring memories and thoughts of home, fun, love, etc., but in fact, we're more open in our *feelings* toward these specific times. It may seem like a trick, but it's just bringing to the surface all those things that we feel.

In fact, you could always spot holiday symbols, ideas, or traditions that will bring out our feelings, but seeing them from a new perspective is what makes the work fresh, evocative, and different from the usual effort. It's also the stuff of "nuance". Look at Picasso, Monet, van Gogh or, most of all, Mary Cassatt. See how they make their work evoke feelings in you.

So, if you want to start getting better recognition in shows, keep using your best technique, but try my little game, and select a word. Be honest, brave, and a bit like a therapist. Tell us (in watercolor) how you *feel* about it.

Rules, Rules, Rules!

A student of mine, who is on her way to being a really good painter, said that her mind was awhirl with "rules for painting". It was too much! She had been struggling, trying to measure every brushstroke against the Principles of Design, expecting each painting to have superlative Gradation, Repetition, Alternation, Balance, Dominance, Unity, Contrast, and Harmony. I said to her, "Chill out. These aren't rules anyway."

This is like expecting your child to be an "A" student in every subject. If it happens, it's great, but if it doesn't, we should be happy with any good grade the child gets and support improvement.

The real use of these Principles (which, by the way, vary with each writer/teacher) is in *your* critique of your work, both as it develops and after it's finished. With their continued use you'll find you're using them as you go, and eventually by instinct rather than rote. Most art *rules* don't mean much to me - formulaic art is just above "paint by numbers" on my art scale. *Rules* just aren't comfortable around artists, and vice versa.

We should study and listen and learn from those who know, but to be a slave to someone's rules is not a good way to be creative. The Principles of Design stay the same, however.

Polly Hammett has only one rule for painting; "If you keep your water on the right, keep your coffee on the left!"

You can make your own rules, too.

Searchers

I sure enjoyed a recent presenter's show-and-tell. She's got the stuff, alright, and makes no bones about fancy philosophy or secret methods. She just does whatever has worked for her before, and isn't afraid of experimentation to find new methods, even if they're unorthodox, with exciting results. I also appreciated her moving along, not disappointed because one or another application didn't exactly work for her, but keeping the search going for something that would work.

There are two kinds of abstract artists; "searchers", who start applying paint and keep working until something that they like appears, and "planners", who have a plan for what they want (often with very complete studies), and translate that into the final painting. Both of these, and all varieties between, are valid ways to work. The first, searching, is very reliant on the medium itself. It's hard to go over transparent watercolor many times without making a big brown mess of it. This is why most transparent watercolor abstracts are done from a plan. That said, some people *do* search with watercolor, and do a great job of it, and some people paint planned abstractions with acrylic. But acrylic paint, because it can be used as opaque or transparent, is a good way to paint until something comes forward because you can paint over and over the same areas, and leave no sign of what went before. You can also paint over an existing painted area with thinned color, and end up with a third color (this is called glazing).

My pal Virginia Cobb is a searcher. I've watched her move through a beautiful abstract in a few hours, using watercolor, gouache, ink, acrylic, and all the while voicing her process to students. She finds shapes that remind her of birds, people, personal symbols, etc., and explains that they all add to her work. Mary Todd Beam is another amazing abstractionist, and is equally exploratory and experimental (and what a great storyteller!)

Nonetheless, I feel just as happy plodding through one of my over-planned watercolor abstracts. There's a certain joy in accomplishing something you've invested a lot of time and activity in. I start with the real thing (fruit, vegetables, etc.) and draw them carefully to get the feel of what they're made like. Then I cut them apart and draw the parts carefully. Then I study composition. I choose patterns for backgrounds. I sketch and overlay sketches with tracing paper to "get it right" value-wise and shape-wise, etc., etc. That's a lot of work for any painting, but I like the results. And in spite of the intense study, I seem to be able to get a pretty fresh looking product most every time. Maybe from painting intuitively, but keeping the studies at hand as reference only, not to copy.

I guess my point is that it is ok to use your own methods to arrive at the finish line happy. There is no hard and fast rule for how you do it (just like everything else in art), and you're free to make it up as you go. There are some who like the journey more than the destination. There are some who like the opposite. There are some who like both. Those who like neither would probably be happier not being in a studio.

Learn what you like and you'll keep doing it until you do it well. You'll accept the stuff you don't like, learn to work around it, or do without it. The good news is there's no rule. From throwing paint at the paper to showing every hair on the gnat, it's up to you. So if anyone ever says, "This is the ONLY way to do this," it's time to put away your palette, go home, and prove they're wrong.

Go Figure!

I love figures, figure painting, and painted figures. From Michelangelo to Andy Warhol, they all fascinate me. My mom, a talented artist, painted them and so I grew up with them around me in various states of undress, body type, and pose. I guess it stuck, because when I took art classes in the seventies they were figure classes – expressive figures to be exact. And I still paint those to this day.

Students often ask me how to paint figures. A good question, I say, but I don't have an easy answer, because the type of figure depends on your goal for the painting. If you're painting a street scene and it needs figures to make it look real, indicate scale, and activate your painting, they can be very general, even minimally detailed. If your painting is about people (a couple on a bench, girls on the beach, a few people at a café table, etc.), they must be carefully drawn and painted because they have to look like people. Their faces might not be so important as their bodies and how they're proportioned, delineated, what they're doing, and how they fit into the spirit of the painting. Like everything else in art, asking a simple question almost always requires a complicated answer. But let's try to simplify this one.

If you put figures in your painting, use the old news reporter technique: who, how, what, where, and why. <u>Who</u> is it – a farmer in the field or a statue? <u>How</u> are they colored, directed, sized? Remember, every shape has its role to play in a painting. Are they running, standing, scratching, carrying, sitting, leaning or <u>what</u>? Shapes can be active or passive. <u>Where</u> are they <u>located</u>? They are shapes as much as a tree, table or cloud and can balance or unbalance a composition. <u>Why</u> are they there? For balance, realism, scale, activity, color? (I left out "when", because that's a personal issue.)

Suddenly the entire question is a complex of knotty issues. And beyond that, we have our own built-in responses to figures. A juror at the Watercolor Art Society - Houston annual national show told me that when you put a figure in a scene everyone looks at the figure first. When the figure is prominent in the painting everyone looks at its face. If small scale figures are in a group, no definition of body is required, just heads, legs some gender indication and some color changes. We don't care as long as we know they have a reason to be there. But the closer we are, the more we want to know about each one.

I find that a few traditional approaches have helped me to get figures right. I recommend you follow these too:

- Learn some basics from good books or workshops. These basics can include stick figures, basic proportions, keeping figures in perspective and in scale, and finding simple ways to indicate activity.

- Find a book or DVD that has simple ways to indicate figures with a brush. Calligraphy can count when you're making basic figures. (See Skip Lawrence's DVD)

- Use contour drawing for figures from life. It gives you complete shapes and teaches careful observation (See *Drawing on The Right Side of The Brain* by Betty Edwards). It works for Charles Reid, and Polly Hammett so why not for you?

- Learn to use stick figures, but the kind with shoulders and hips. You'll find as you proceed that these can save you a lot of time and effort when you need a figure and don't want to find a model and position him/her to paint.

- As you go through magazines and newspapers (do they still have those?) cut out figures you like/need, etc. to base your figures on. Warning: do not copy these precisely or you could get in trouble with the copyright folks.

- I've also heard from some who record TV shows and stop them, tape a piece of tracing paper on the screen and draw the figures they like. Once again, be careful! Somebody owns every image on the screen.

- My final suggestion is the one everybody hates – practice, practice, practice.

These suggestions are not meant to imply that you

should not take figure drawing or figure painting classes. On the contrary, you'll learn a whole lot more that way than you can with the above. But for the busy, complicated lives we have today, not all of us can take classes or afford them, so maybe the other suggestions will help you get the level of figure definition you need to make your paintings work for you.

And, there are different kinds of figure painting. I do expressive figures, which are all about distortion, emphasis, color, pattern, etc., but not at all about slavish accuracy in drawing.

There is simply a lot to learn about figures and about painting in general. To learn it well takes time, experimentation, courage, repetition, knowledge and critique. The good part is you can learn and keep on learning. And isn't that what it takes to get better?

Surface Interest - A Whole New World

Q: *"How do I get more interest into my flat, dull looking painted shapes?"*

Here are some techniques for finding what I call *surface interest:*

-<u>Try changing papers.</u> Using smooth paper (hot press or illustration board) will create puddles and inconsistencies.

- <u>Let the paint do the work.</u> Put the paint on pure in hue and let it mix on the paper surface.

- <u>Dab the finished paint</u> (while wet or semi-wet) with paper, Kleenex, sponge or other textural material. You can vary the dabbing frequency for different looks.

- <u>Lift out your lights.</u> You can cut stencils out of mylar or acetate, then sponge over the dry paint to lift specific light shapes. (Careful! You may lift off the paper surface, too!)

- <u>Gradate your shape colors</u> from warm to cool, from light to dark or intense to pastel.

- <u>Flow granulating pigments</u> on top of others to give more character to the various parts of a large shape.

- <u>You can add salt, sand, various materials</u> (rubber bands, string, wax, etc.) while the paint is wet to vary the apparent texture.

-<u>Last but not least-don't forget the basic elements.</u> You can always introduce texture and/or pattern with your brush, stamps, or stencils, and still not lose the shape!

For various applications to create surface interest, see *Painting In Watercolor* from the *Artists Handbook Series*, or just about any "how to" watercolor book. Jeanne Dobie's fine book, *Making Color Sing,* offers excellent advice for granulated color and washes in general.

Don't forget -- the most important ingredient in art is taste! Don't go overboard, but <u>do</u> <u>try</u> it all!

Abstract Thoughts

I recently started painting abstracts again. I usually wait until the spirit moves me, and blast off with a really unclear notion of what I want to paint, thinking I should be shouting "Freedom, freedom!" Alas, I don't know from what.

The reason is that there are, I've observed, two different approaches to painting abstract art. The first is with forethought. The second is without. I have used both. They both work to some extent for me, but I think I get better paintings with the former.

A good friend of mine works off the most basic and somewhat imaginary grid systems to find a structure, which she then embellishes, fills out, paints over, and does what she would have done without a grid. Don't tell her I said so, but it's really just a way to get started and get into the painting.

Others, notably the late, great Carl Molno, work from sketches or layouts, and set up the entire painting to be done based on a preconceived notion, even to the color, size and shapes of the main subject matter. Which, you might ask, is better? As with every question about painting, it depends on the painter.

I tend to be *not* the free, wild painting fool I want to think I am, but much more deliberative and possibly analytical, so having a minimal sort of sketch does me well. I consider how the painting should look when it's finished, I allow myself to move beyond the basic structure if I need to, but I always have some specific mental image of what I want the painting to be when it's done. When it gets there, hallelujah! It's done. But then…when I paint without a pre-plan…(and what is a *pos*t-plan, anyhow?) it is a difficult, challenging, unforeseeable task which requires changing, adding and blocking out things to make it work. That's why I paint in acrylic when I have no sketch.

If the work is an abstraction of real things (still life is a favorite subject) I like to work in transparent watercolor. I start with very simple, but accurate sketches, because that helps me understand the shapes involved. I'll do value and color studies, at least enough to get a concept going. I sometimes do overlays with tracing paper, maybe six or eight until I have the composition and value where I want them. Then I paint.

Non-objective abstracts, however, are a different story. I start with Aquarius paper coated with randomly different colors and matte medium on top of that. I paint a big shape or two and see how they look. I fool around endlessly looking for good composition, color and shape to pull the sheet together, and no sooner have I changed one thing than I have to change something else. See why I don't use transparent watercolor for this method? But it's fun, and a challenge to see what I can come up with. Acrylic can be manipulated for tons of texture and effects, and can cover up stuff you want to change. You can paint real or abstract in the same painting if you want, and it always dries the same as you put it down.

If you want to try abstract, but haven't done any yet, try reading Virginia Cobb's book, *Discovering the*

Inner Eye. It's a great handbook for abstract painting, and although it's no longer in print, you can still get a used copy for less than $40.00 on Amazon.

You never know, it might get you on a new, but more abstract road to fame.

Fully Equipped

I was watching a movie thriller named "Don't Say A Word" on TV today, in which a bad guy attacked a woman whose leg was in a cast. She had her painting stuff at bedside to use during recovery, and she stabbed him with a watercolor wash brush with a chiseled handle. My first thought was, "Is that a Kolinsky sable?" Which brings us to my subject for today – equipment: wants and needs.

Because no two of us work the same way, we all have our own preferences for equipment. We may use similar techniques, but because of anatomical, experience or training differences, we do them differently. So the great machine of commerce has leapt in to provide us with an unprecedented array of brushes, paints, papers, etc. Some of us like to spray or spatter, some like to flow washes, some like painting them on with a brush. Some of us like doing big work with small brushes, some, small areas with big brushes.

Through the years I have bought, found, been given, and swapped brushes. I have done the same with paints, palettes, bags, portfolios, paper, water jugs, painting boards, and you-name-it. I've gone on buying sprees after a nice sale, gone crazy in retail stores, and been the first to ask the surviving spouse of a deceased fellow painter what she planned to do with his watercolor stuff. I know no shame in this pursuit. But I have calmed in my waning years to always think before I buy, and I have a few questions and suggestions for you to think about before you impulse-buy yourself right out of house and home or have to rent a warehouse to store equipment.

Questions that can help you are:

- Will this fit the way I paint and the subject matter I want to paint?

- Will this improve my painting? Will it be easy to lift and carry?

- How will this fit with other colors/brushes/papers I already use?

- Do I already have some of these I've never used?

I suggest that you who are new to the watercolor world try just what all experts suggest in their books. The traditional starters are two flat and two round brushes, upper/mid-level cost; tube paints, the best you can afford, in a minimum of hues (I recommend a warm and cool of primaries and later, secondaries), a palette you can cover and wash easily, and Arches or other premium paper to paint on.

For those who've been in the game a while I suggest you go to a convention or two (Florida Watercolor Society is a good one) and try out brushes and paints. Take your time, and think about how you work as a painter. Full arm, wrist or finger painter? All are valid styles, but if you drop a few hundred on brushes, you'll really feel bad if they don't suit you. Stuff will flock to your paint bag; so don't be in a hurry to buy it anyhow.

Other good ways to learn about materials:

Ask experienced painters what they use and why. If you paint with friends, ask them if you can try their stuff. Swap off with them for a while (be sure you and they know how to use whatever you are trying out). When you buy a brush ask for some water to wet it and check it out on a piece of paper. Work out the sizing in the hair so you can really know its characteristics. You can buy sample packs of most watercolor papers, and if you go to conventions, special sales, or company-sponsored demonstrations you can often get samples for free.

I've been down the equipment road for a long time, and I've found that everyone's choices of brands and types of equipment are personal and always changing, having as much to do with what they like as what makes sense.

So should yours. And remember; if you break your leg, keep a brush within reach.

A Space of Your Own

A lot of what I discuss in these articles is what and why we paint. But an important factor in any creative endeavor is the environment for creating. Not that one's surroundings are the exclusive reason for doing quality work, but the place we paint in can sure contribute to or take a toll on our desire and interest in our work.

Many of us work in watercolor because we love it, and we aspire to greater things with it. But working is very difficult if we're not able to fully focus on what we do. Thus, we not only need a space to work in, we need a space that works for us. Some criteria include a space that:

-Is your space only

-Is used only for you to paint in

-Is a pleasant place to paint in, and

-Can provide the technical needs for creating your art

Now, I'm sure I'll hear a great sigh from all who read this and don't have a studio, or one they are happy with (let alone love), but let's take a look at the above criteria one by one.

Having a space for you alone, means you'll need to let others in your life know that it's YOUR space and stick with it! That means no fishing gear, old toys, and other stuff that nobody knows what to do with taking up all your painting space, not a place for them to have a private conversation, etc. So others who support you painting will have to learn that this is not a space for them, but for YOU. The sole purpose of the space is your painting and your art associated activities.

The space should only be used by one person (unless you're blessed with a space big enough for others to paint with you) and that person is YOU. That way you aren't distracted, and can focus fully on making art.

The painting space should be a pleasant one so you'll want to be there at every opportunity or at scheduled times to paint. Since "pleasant" is personally interpreted, the degree of creature comfort and eye appeal is up to you. But functionality is also a major requirement of a painting space, and when it clashes with visual appeal or other personal dictates, function becomes a major concern.

The technical needs of watercolor painting seem minimal compared to other forms of art-making. Pottery, metal sculpture, print making all seem to take a lot more room than watercolor. Not that watercolor can't take up a lot of room too, but generally, working even on larger works won't require more than that needed by the artist to sit/stand while painting, a place for the paper being painted on, a place to view the work while in progress, and room for storage of your supplies, works in progress and finished pieces.

Technical needs are often difficult to accommodate in a limited space. Along with electric lighting, paper, paint, and water, we might need a computer, a paper cutter, north daylight or daylight lamps, both document and work files, as well as phones, visitor space, air conditioning and even a space for soaking and/or drying paintings, etc. These requirements are thought to be basic to the medium, but many of us can get by with minimal space; a desk a card table, a small space in a kitchen where you can work-after all, the real work is very basic. We mix the paint with water, and brush it on to paper.

So are there other opportunities? Yes. If you can, joining with others to buy, rent or renovate an already available space can be a great way for several artists to find the space, atmosphere, and the facilities adaptable to painting. Another way is to find a facility that already rents space to individual artists (these are often sponsored by arts organizations.) This way you can have your own place that meets all the above requirements, but still allows access to other artists. It isn't cheap, however.

Since you're creative, you might well put together a league, society, or cooperative that can sponsor such facilities. Or re-do any extra space you have to make it your painting place. I always tell my students "You need to have a place where you paint." If it's not a room, it can be a table, a desk or a nook in your family room. Just find a spot that's our own, and use it for your art, and ONLY YOUR art - and keep moving forward!

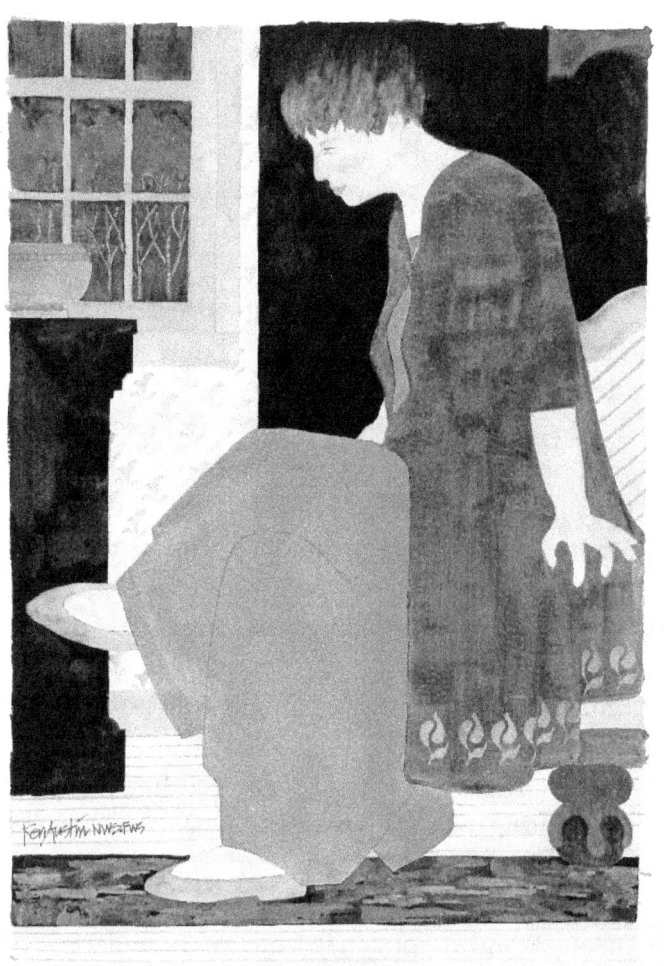

Contemplation

3
LEARNING CURVES

Workshop Tips

I've taken workshops for over 20 years. For the past four years I've attended the Spring Maid Watercolor Workshops in Myrtle Beach, SC., pretty much the ultimate workshop venue. There are talented local artists teaching everywhere. This month I want to give you some tips on workshops:

1. *You can learn more from workshops than you can by yourself.* Workshops may seem intimidating but there is no need for concern. Most teachers are prepared for ALL skill levels.

2. *Relax and do what you can.* Don't be afraid to fail - <u>you will</u>. You won't have the time, or ability to absorb

enough to do a beautiful painting. You are there to *learn specifics from an accomplished artist*. She or he will teach you one thing at a time, not how to paint a masterpiece.

3. *Concentrate on achieving the lesson objective.* It's a class, not a contest or race, so do your best to work at a pace that you can enjoy, and <u>keep a positive attitude</u>.

4. *"If you were a genius you'd probably know it by now."* Skip Lawrence's quip is true. Paint to learn, not for praise. The teacher won't be impressed by your painting. He or she will be impressed by awarding your painting a prize in a national competition after you've learned to apply her or his lessons.

This year at Myrtle Beach, Virginia Cobb recounted some students who, because of her workshops, blossomed with abstract and expressive work; names like Mary Hughey Phillis, Mary Todd Beam, Carol Barnes, and others we know from their prizewinning paintings, great teaching and beautiful books. None of them would have been what they are today without Virginia's workshops.

So take a workshop and share the joy of learning with your painting buddies! You (and the art world) will be better for it!

Travel Plans

Way back when I was much younger, visiting two dear American friends who lived in England, we went to the Cambridge Folk Festival for the weekend. We went by rail, and returning home by train, we missed our transfer from the main line to the local, ending up stranded in a tiny village named March – almost midnight - with no place to stay.

The kind stationmaster agreed to let us sleep in the waiting room, but had to lock us in for the night. We played and sang for an hour or so, talked of the festival, then, exhausted, lay down on the pew-like seats, slept the night through and returned home the next morning. Of all the things I did on my six-month trip to Europe, that night in March still is my strongest, happiest memory - a case for the journey being more important than the destination, or "enjoying the process".

Some of you may never have taken a workshop, but I have taken quite a few, and I think much of what I've learned about art has come from these intensive courses. It all depends on the instructor's teaching skills and your determination and receptiveness to their teaching. If there's a shortfall somewhere, you're the one who knows it first. And without a "money-back guarantee", you'll have to chalk it up to learning. But *do not* take it to mean workshops can't work for you. You've got to be selective and do some research to see if the instructor is "your" kind of teacher. None of them I've ever met feels they're immune to failure. So if you feel it wasn't a good experience, you might just have caught one of their "bad days".

We need to understand that instructors are not infallible (your devoted author excepted) and also that sometimes students just can't get their heads around what the lessons are. Sometimes you'd like to paint like the teacher, but not all instructors teach their painting methods. Some do, some don't. And even if they do, maybe you just can't paint in that instructor's style.

Perhaps the journey is even more important than the destination, but I still take journeys to get somewhere specific. By and large I've achieved that in art, but the destination keeps changing the further I travel, and I keep getting way more than I bargained for. Admittedly, as in England, I've had some great experiences along the way.

What about you? What's your destination? How do you want to get there? Choose carefully, then sit back and enjoy the trip, no matter where it goes. You just might end up with an unforgettable experience - spending your own night in March.

Creative Catastrophe Management

Do we learn from our failures or from our successes? Well, the answer for me is, YES! And do we ever learn from the unexpected? Only if we do it right (to quote Woody Allen).

All this relates to my experiences teaching workshops. And, believe me, they are all different! I've taught classes where the students were so happy that they took me out for drinks and dinner; others learned more in in our few days together than in years before, and in several they asked when, *when-oh!-when* would I be back (not up to me, but the vagaries of the program directors). And then there were ... *the others.*

Like the figure class without models ("Can't we just use newspapers?"), or the one where the lights went out for a half day ("Oh, it does that every time!"), or the one where the class rebelled on the last day because they just wanted to finish the work they'd already started ("Well, we're just going to work on these."), and most recently, the one where the teaching space wasn't available ("It appears, we've got a little problem..."), so we had three days outdoors in a park pavilion, no mirror, in August. Or there's the one where they changed the workshop subject just before I left Orlando ("We just decided this will really be a better subject").

How did I manage? The same way I do with painting. I just tried to maintain an open mind toward finding solutions and positives in these surprises. So, I guess they all worked out - <u>I had a good time</u>, as did my students. And I ask you, what better training for watercolor than sharpening your sensitivity to "happy accidents"?

Here's what I think is transferable to painting from these experiences:

- DON'T PANIC - you can deal with this

- If you can't remove the accident, look for a solution which hides/incorporates the change, or even *features* it.

- Remember, it's only one painting out of hundreds (I hope!)

- Recognize that even our most deeply held dreams don't always turn out.

- Remember that YOU are responsible for the painting, nobody/nothing else.

- If disaster is inevitable, accept it and find a way to laugh about it - you can always start over!

The Healthy Art Exercises

Well, here it comes - another set of things you have to do to keep healthy. At least to keep your art healthy. What's healthy art? It's all personal, of course, but to me art is healthy if it :

- Raises questions about things we normally take for granted

- Presents new ideas of beauty

- Moves us beyond the accepted norm of what is beautiful

-Perfectly expresses the artist's ideas through a singular creativity

- Shows the common as uncommonly beautiful

- Maintains (or increases) an attraction over time for a personal aesthetic

And unhealthy if it:

- Presents the obvious in an obvious way

- Accepts clichés as a way to beauty

- Does not make a clear statement about at least something

- Doesn't relate to an audience

- Takes itself too seriously

- Is predictable

- Isn't deeper than a plaid shirt

- Doesn't interest the audience (mainly me!)

"O great teacher", you say, "what exercises can we do to make our art healthy?" The answer is: Do whatever ISN'T normal for you, and ask yourself:

- How can I make this mess something I like and make it express that to others?

- What skills, traits, character, experiences, techniques and feelings can I express that are mine? How can I make them personal?

And on the more practical side:

Assign yourself a painting project once a week (or month or day depending on your workload) doing something you've never done before. If it's colors you don't use (all intense color) or materials (Yupo paper) or value (blacks and whites), you'll learn what you can and can't achieve and carry the achievable forward with you. You can begin to discover how interesting the mundane can become if YOU REALLY LIKE IT.

And you can make it an exciting, integral part of all you paint.

One way is to make an assignment list. Do the assignments one at a time and then get a friend to critique them with you. You'll be surprised at how you can advance when you latch onto a good one! So keep on exercising and add muscles to your art - don't paint flabby anymore!

The View From the Other Side

The side of workshops that students don't know includes the organization, research, methodology, and communication planning required in order to teach any subject. And since there are no class prerequisites, knowing the students' levels is virtually impossible in workshops.

So the teacher's job is to provide instruction on a difficult subject to people who vary in ability - and in a way that lets everybody show their progress, increase their skill and understanding, become better artists, get a good deal for their money, and have a good time as well. No small order. In other words, to teach workshops you have to be a Rhodes Scholar, psychologist, and class clown all wrapped up in one. Those I ain't. Well, maybe the class clown.

My favorite workshop teachers are the ones who give students information that is: *Understandable, Doable, Repeatable, Interesting,* and, if possible, *Fun*. I try to do that too.

I've taken lots of workshops over the years, from all kinds of teachers. Most were good for me, but a few were great. You'll probably find the same if you take workshops, which I whole-heartedly support.

Some tips to keep in mind:

Check out the teacher any way you can; websites, student reviews, other members, other sponsors' newsletters, etc.

<u>Be sure the subject is one you really want to know more about;</u> if it's a portraits workshop, it probably won't help you on figures.

<u>You may be exhausted or exhilarated (or both!);</u> most good teachers have a lot to offer and they'll pour it on heavy.

<u>Be sure you won't regret the expenditure;</u> worrying about how much you're spending will impede your learning, and make you self-conscious about whether you're doing well.

<u>Don't strive to be the best in the class;</u> workshops are learning opportunities, not contests. I tell my work-shoppers that everyone gets an "A" in my classes. Corny, yes, but it reinforces the notion that *we're there to learn, not to produce* - important in maintaining a student's self-image.

For most local or regional art societies, the primary goal for a good workshop is education. To that end we've sponsored workshops since our inception. They are our one opportunity for learning that you can't get locally from other sources. Your participation in them is what keeps them going. I hope you'll keep it up, or, if you've never participated, try one. Believe me, you'll love what it does for you. And that's not the class clown talking!

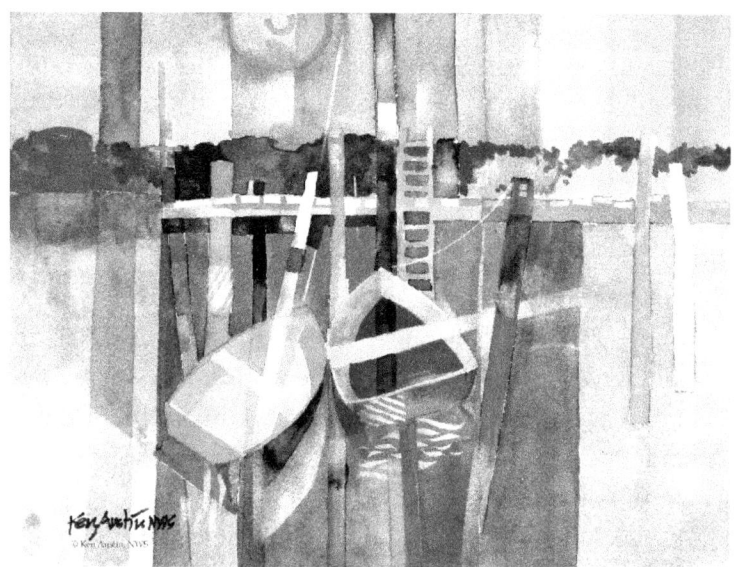

Red Boat/Green Boat

Apprehension Tension

It's September, another year another beer. Wait, this isn't college is it? Of course the answer is "No!", but strangely, the old habits, expectations, and negative thoughts still hang on like little bugs ready to bore into our brains and gnaw and gnaw and...well, we don't need to go psycho, but we still have some inhibitions about starting new things. It seems that the New Year is celebrated at the wrong time. September is when everything really gets hopping, and watercolor is no exception. So, let's talk about this "new" year and see if we can get somewhere with it.

I have resolved to paint more plein air, specifically every time our CFWS paint-out group does (given weather and my cranky old body). The reason is that I haven't done that in years, and I should do it because, (a) it's a way to force me to look at what I'm painting and get it down in a couple of hours, (b) I need to start moving through paintings faster, and (c) I just love (most of) the paintings I get from it.

My wife and I were recently in Hendersonville, N.C. for a two-week vacation, and I had vowed to get out and paint there. What a fine place to paint - great weather, cool days, beautiful scenery, all the painting and sketching material I could hope for, and so I embarked on a new and fruitful painting vacation. And how many paintings did I do?

<u>One third!</u>

Those of you who know me and have seen me paint are aware that I *can* fill up a quarter sheet pretty fast and have a presentable if not sensational painting (OK, just kidding about the "sensational") but I didn't even get that far! Why? Well, I was overcome by the idea of having to do a painting in a few hours, then maybe having to take it to my studio and finish it up, trying to do the same level of plein air painting I did eight or ten years ago. So I just kept driving, finding some wonderful things to photograph, and stayed entranced by that beautiful countryside flying by my car windows. By 4:30 each afternoon it was raining anyhow, so then I couldn't paint and had to head back to our cottage for a glass of wine and recitals of what we'd both done that day.

Now the time was, I could sit at the beach and sketch a layout, begin painting, get ¾ done, finish it off with an hour in my studio, send it to a gallery and sell it – and a darn good one, too, if I say so myself.

So, what was the reason for the hesitation, the feeling of incompetence? Because, based on my past, I had very high expectations of myself.

I once read that the great classical guitarist, Julian Bream sat down early every morning and began his practice with the first thing he learned to do on the guitar; placing his index finger on a string at the first fret, plucking the string, then putting his middle finger on the second fret and plucking the string again, etc. He went on to the next exercise he'd learned, then the next, and by 4:00 PM he could be heard rehearsing his current concert list. Dedication by the best is what made them the best. They also have high expectations of themselves; the difference is they work at it. They practice. They start their sessions with what they first learned, and move through those to the act of creation. What I had done was different. I started with the expectation of a fine finished product, and forgot that I hadn't practiced the process of getting that product. Or, simply put, *I hadn't stayed in shape.*

There's a lot to be said for staying in shape, no matter what sort of activity you're doing; cooking, carpentry, sewing, running, swimming, etc., really just about anything that involves more than a single simple repetitive act. In fact any complex act that you expect some particular outcome from probably takes practice. Not only do you profit from practice by doing better work, you can do it faster, and enjoy the outcome more. But there are some things to remember.

You won't master sail boating by rowing a canoe. You won't master portrait painting by painting florals. You can't master outdoor painting by only painting in your studio. And, it's good to always start with the basics when you're going to paint, warming up with your brushes and paints and some practice strokes and washes on mistake paper. But one way to be sure you get into or back into something is to make a public announcement.

So I hereby do officially declare that, through my love of the outdoor experience which I, through the years, have generously shared with other painters, several cows, a couple of alligators and countless flies and mosquitoes and through my belief that targeted endeavor is the way to success, I, Ken Austin, NWS, FWS, FLAG do hereby affirm that I will revisit the wonderful world of plein air to which end I shall practice regularly, in order to stay in shape.

And you know, you could too, if you wanted.

But if I should fail, I take it all back.

What Now?

I watched Pat Weaver work her brush magic last meeting, and found myself envying her self-assurance, her expert brushwork, her solid working foundation for her art, and (mainly) her consistency in what and how she paints.

I just can't seem to maintain one style for more than five or six paintings, which is a curse and a blessing. I get to enjoy painting different stuff (abstract, representational, figures, florals, expressive style, landscapes, seascapes, etc., etc.), but also have to paint slowly and make a lot of decisions which aren't automatic. Pat's painting is automatic, with decisions formed by her style almost as much as by her goals for any one painting. I deliberate about every color, what subjects I'm tackling, or how to get my vision on paper. I can paint fast enough outside, while inside I get so deliberative it's scary. But you know what? It's fine with me. I learn a lot with each painting I do, and it usually carries over.

In a workshop, Skip Lawrence passed out a self-questionnaire titled "What Kind Of Artist Am I?". The idea was not to catalog yourself, but to give some insight into what you really liked and so choose wisely to further your goals toward that end. We didn't have to return them, but that didn't prevent him toward the end of the week from asking me if I was *ever* going to paint the same way twice. I answered that it wasn't important to me.

It's valid if it is *important* to you, though, and it's a good thing to discuss with yourself and others you paint with. Who are your art heroes? Are you an impressionist, expressionist, realist, abstractionist, or what? Are you in this for a profit? Are you comfortable with techniques that your chosen label may require and vice versa? Do you see movement towards your goals? If not, what may be holding you back? How can you improve? Do you need a change, and if so, change what and how?

Asking these questions never hurts. We can get lost or on the wrong trail pretty easily, so keep in mind what you want out of art, and don't be afraid to try new things if they lead you toward your goal. Self-challenge is important in building confidence - and we all can use some of that.

By Their Questions

I "demoed" at the Art League of Orange County recently, and the crowd was responsive and generous with questions and compliments. I just did my usual schtick, which is to talk a lot and paint a little.

The focus was on how I paint a painting. I chose one which had been arduous, involving design decisions, color decisions, size decisions, etc. And when the time came to actually put it on paper, ready to paint, I used my little Mac to blow up sketches, dissect them, study them, rearrange them and, finally, to print them out to final size. Then I transferred it to the final sheet, painted it and, unfortunately, didn't sell it. . . yet. They had lots of questions about my process, which I answered as best I could, then I talked briefly about value, color and composition, the holy trinity of visual art, did some illustrations, and left.

But, "by their questions you shall know them" is a good paraphrase for students anywhere, and this group's questions were great - "Do you mean I have to use a computer to do good paintings?" - "Do you always have to use intense color to have a good painting?" – "How does the paper affect your processes?"

I did my best with the answers, but afterward I realized one of the most important things about demos, classes, workshops, etc., is that they make me think hard about what I'm doing and how I do it when I paint. So, it's a good thing to be asked those questions, and to figure out the questions I should be asking myself when I paint. So, what are those questions?

They might change as time goes on (doesn't everything?). But for now, the questions occur as I work through the painting, from beginning to end, and they're different at each phase. Those phases I'll call Inception, Development, Finalizing, and Production. I'll just discuss Inception for now.

Inception includes sketches, ideas, photos, or whatever you might be using as a basis for a painting. You might use free-form sketches and "find" compositions in them, or maybe you have a preconception of what you want the painting to be and try to develop that idea with sketches, photos, etc.

I use both/either method. Sometimes sketches work, sometimes not. Like everything, you must make decisions about the inception items, and roll with them. If they don't work, you're only out a little time and a little paper.

I hope you can get out and take a workshop now and then. It will greatly enhance your understanding of painting and of your own process. And don't be afraid to ask questions. You and your teacher will be glad you did!

What I Did Last Summer

In June I took a workshop with great artist and longtime friend, Virginia Cobb. It seems odd, but sometimes we don't know friends until we see them at their very best. Not across the table with a glass of wine, or embroiled in a little league playoff (both worthwhile endeavors), but seeing them do whatever-it-is that's most important to them.

Virginia and I have known each other for over 30 years, and I have taken her workshop before, but this time seemed special, because it was, literally, on her own turf (her home) outside of Santa Fe, NM. I learned more because I had more direct contact with her. I finally "got" her approach to painting.

Virginia is a dedicated abstractionist, so we worked in acrylic on paper. A member of the National Academy of the Arts and a Dolphin Fellow in the American Watercolor Society, she's a straightforward, eloquent woman with a great sense of humor and a talent for giving students confidence in what they produce. As I've said before, there are two directions for artists in abstract art. One is to construct a painting based on sketches or designs from an original idea. The other is to begin painting, and find the subject as you go. Virginia's quest is the latter.

This is the ultimate, unnerving, skydiving, near-death experience for me, a dedicated sketcher, studier, and obsessive detailer in abstract painting. I start by drawing, then abstract treatments in thumbnail, then select the best, then do color studies, then paint them, yada-yada (whew!). In the workshop I did a painting a day (others did two). No time to be obsessive.

My results weren't great (but, ahem, acceptable), still I learned how to *find* the main stuff of an abstract (AKA the subject). It is deceptively simple – remove what is not contributing to the painting while improving what you want to keep.

For all of us who are permanently conjoined to our watercolors, change literally ain't easy. We don't have the luxury of overpainting as with acrylics or oils. How do you do that in watercolor? Verrrrrrry carefully! Slow down – the Sistine Chapel wasn't painted in a day, and you might not be able to do a painting in a day either. So work on two or three at a time. Try out ideas on tracing paper over the original (good for value studies). Think about what you are doing – not in technique, but design. You can lift, erase, repaint, overpaint, and glaze, using varying degrees of opacities to work with your existing paintings. In fact, you don't have to limit these approaches to abstract paintings – you might want to make it a habit to use them on anything you do. As we used to say in city planning: "Change is inevitable. Embrace it!"

Of course you'll have to try something new (ouch!). But meanwhile: keep your brush wet!

Much Ado About Nothing

For those of you who don't know, I'm a banjo picker. Not that yuk-a-duk stuff, but real American Bluegrass, and some old-time for ear relief. I say this to explain why a friend of mine loaned me a banjo CD by Mary Cox, a terrific player from Tallahassee. In the liner notes she said she stayed up late one night learning all the notes NOT to play in the key of "C". Then she woke up and composed a song made up of those taboo notes, and recorded it - in the key of "C".

There's something intrinsically artistic about using the "wrong" stuff and getting something good from it. It's rebellious, inquisitive, and challenging, all of which is good stuff for art people. Don't we like to play games for those same reasons? And besides, it keeps the Art Police in their proper places.

Untrained artists get right out of wrong by using whatever is available and workable to express themselves. If you don't believe it, go to the Menello Museum in Orlando (or any good museum) and check it out.

What about those crazy, rebellious Impressionists and Modernists...I love those early paintings by Vuillard where he used all pattern, no line, to define his shapes. And the impressionists leaving parts of the canvas unpainted to express a clean, pure feeling for the overall scene. And how about Picasso showing the outsides AND the insides of violins in a single painting? At some point, someone really important must have said to each of them, "Hey! You can't do that!"

Well, of course, you CAN do that! Just try something you've never considered. Use an odd shaped scrap of paper for a composition. Try painting with your eyes blindfolded. Try painting opposite-handed. Try painting all in mud. Try painting on some surface that rejects the paint (well, Yupo does that already) or absorbs it too much. All of these can yield surprising (if not great) results, and open up new techniques which are unique to your style and challenging to the general assessment of what art is…and what it ain't.

Just keep an open mind and it's just possible you'll learn more about the power of what you DON'T paint if that's what you DO paint.

Obfuscating Argot?

This is about why we use all these confusing new words and terms for painting. We read articles every day which talk about pigment, elements, principles, saturation, hue, intensity, mid-tones, etc. We take workshops and lessons where our instructors discuss temperature, key, activity and other words borrowed or created for watercolor painting alone. They may seem confusing, and unnecessary for some, and unreasonable for others.

The reason for their use, in a word (pun!), is professionalism. Every profession has its own specific language. A surgeon saying, "Pass me that cutting 'dealie', please," is a potentially dangerous experience for a surgical patient, and so (1) common courtesy takes a back seat to expediency ("SCALPEL!"), and, (2) such great precision in speech is used.

In art, and certainly in watercolor, we can remain courteous, but precise speech is just as necessary. When we say, "darker color" the term could mean it's lower on the value scale than an adjacent color or that it's a different color with a lower native value. "Darker hue" or "lower value", however carry precise, and different meanings.

If we learn primarily by doing, we still learn *what* to do through communication. For precision in discussion, and therefore clarity in action, we need to know the language of watercolor.

You can gain this knowledge in different ways. I hand out a glossary of watercolor terms to my students. Books, discussions with others in class and with painting buddies are also great learning sources.

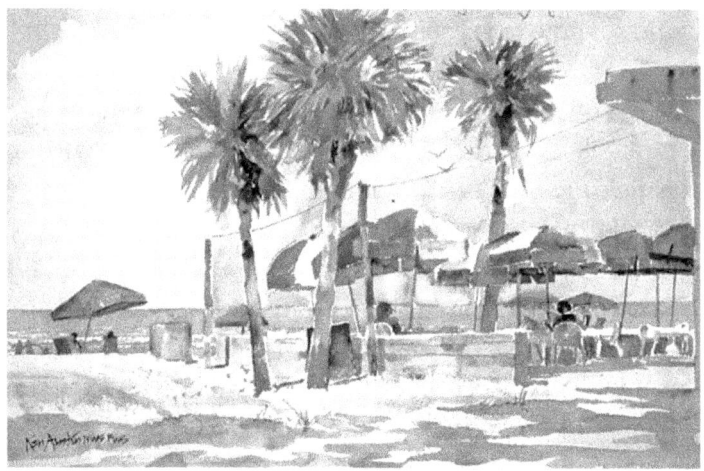

The Breakfast Club

4
MASTERS CLASS

What History Holds

I have a book on art that I really love for its unfailing clarity and clear illustration of the history and development of the visual arts, from prehistoric to the present day. Its title is *Art and Illusion* by E. H. Gombrich, subtitled, "A Study in the Psychology of Pictorial Representation". Gombrich was a professor with chairs at various famous schools, including Oxford, Cambridge, Harvard, Princeton, as well as the University of London. He was a lecturer at many venues on the above titled subject, and this book is an expansion on a lecture series at Princeton in 1956.

I so admire this book because, in addition to being easy reading, it is devoted to a question I've always had – why did the ancient Egyptians depict people in that stiff, formal way, the Romanesque artists in that strange big-eyed, linear style, etc? Prof. Gombrich, in (only?) 400 pages manages to take us through the history of art, but only the part about how artists have represented real things by translating them onto flat surfaces with charcoal, paint, ink, wax, mosaics, etc., and how and why our methods of representation have changed over time.

Gombrich's reasons are varied in hows and whys and, with exceptions of course, he's talking about our Western Civilization's art. What intrigues me most is that his subject, depicting realism in paint, is definitely what all my new students want to do. They invariably want to "paint what they see". What they see isn't what they are able to paint, so they come to teachers and take workshops and classes to learn how to represent what they see on paper. And I do think it's helpful to their development as artists to have them learn as much as they can about how to make watercolor look like the things they want to paint. But learning how to tune a car engine doesn't mean you can be a race driver. And as Gombrich points out, what actually happens is that "what we call seeing is invariably coloured and shaped by our knowledge (or belief) of what we see." His examples include mistaking a fluttering piece of paper for a bird in flight. And when we know our assumption was mistaken we won't see it the same way again.

Since the Impressionists and their claim to "scientific" painting, we've moved farther and farther from what we used to call "brick by brick" painting. That start to the modern movement in art has focused us, as artists, on the feeling/meaning/structure of works instead of how convincingly the artist could represent the real world on a flat surface. It is, in fact, my belief that the visual interest of a work lies as much in involving viewers as it does in telling them what they're looking at. It's harder to understand some Expressionist or Impressionist paintings made with rough dabs than a Renaissance painting made with coats of beautifully applied smooth oils. But we are drawn into finding the solution to the puzzle of the dabs and what it means, what it makes. And even so dedicated a realist as Charles Reid has written a book titled, *Painting What You Want To See.*

My approach to teaching (which I've learned from great teachers) is to offer students a spread of options in painting by focusing on composition, elements and principles of design, and thus learning what their materials and methods are capable of. Most don't have a clue that these class exercises will eventually end up in their paintings and will be welcome additions. The reason I teach this way is that working with composition, elements and principles make their paintings more interesting and involving to the viewer. Are the colors the same as what they see? No, because those colors are boring. Are the shapes the same as they see? No, because those shapes don't make a good design on the sheet. Is the painting interesting or boring? Does it have "personality" or is it like an off-the-shelf poster? Does it speak of you through a personal style or is it trying to look like somebody else's? If the answer is "no", then your brand of realism isn't doing the job. It may look real, but it's not art.

As to the realism aspect in the book, Gombrich's final thought is that if you want to paint a house in the trees by the road, you always have to start with your basic schematic idea of what the colors and shapes are that make a house, a tree, a road. But how you put it on the paper and how you design it are what make you the artist.

Don't forget you are *always* the artist.

What's The Big Deal With Matisse?

Ok, I love Matisse. There, I've said it and I'm proud of it. Why? I'll give you ten reasons although there are more. Here we go:

1. He was easy to understand: Have you seen his paintings of women in flowery dresses with bright patterned wallpaper in the background? They are simple and direct without being childlike, and they focus on a specific feeling of feminine beauty.

2. He loved color: His life was spent deciphering the effects of color on composition, feeling and beauty.

3. He worked hard at art: Matisse worked until his last breath. He had cut a figure from colored paper, looked at it, said "It will do", then died.

4. His paintings were about the painting, not the subject: He said, "When I put a green, it is not grass. When I put a blue, it is not the sky."

5. He was competitive: He had a long and often contentious relationship with Picasso. They argued and tried to outdo each other in new discoveries and applications. The world thought of Matisse as old and out of date, but when he died, Picasso said, "The true master is dead."

6. He loved pattern: His family manufactured textiles, in a textile producing area of France. His paintings sometimes are coated with pattern, and other times an entire wall is stated with one element of a wallpaper pattern.

7. He thought all good paintings should make a good rug: Like textiles he saw paintings as a flat statement on a flat ground, more about shapes than objects.

8. He never followed, he led: Art is often about doing what hasn't been done before. He broke rules, those of others and of his own to find new ways of expression.

9. He sought the simplest forms of expression:
Matisse practiced drawing a lace collar for months, thread for thread until he felt he understood it well enough to paint it with a single undulating stroke - but the right one.

10. He wasn't easy to understand: Many of his paintings, like Beethoven's Quartets are still a source of discovery and discussion among artists and historians. He was a wonderful artist.

Chameleons

If you can't judge a book by its cover, you sure can't tell what people paint by their appearance. In most cases it's because tastes in art are more extreme than tastes in dress or appearance. After all, it's easier to be way out there in paper and paint than in the real world of bills, family, work, etc. But to a great extent we all meet others' expectations in our daily lives, and in the art we produce. We're all programmed to be part of the clan, tribe, family or pack. It keeps us safe. It's hard, even deadly to go it alone.

Once on holiday in New York I saw a Kandinsky retrospective at the Guggenheim. Wassily Kandinsky was a Russian from a wealthy family, with a prestigious position as a law professor. Through his travels to Europe, he was exposed to the "new" art of impressionism. His lifelong love of art overcame his career and he became an artist (the inventor of nonobjective abstraction). This may seem a strange role change, but not in the world of art. Other famous artists were called to give their lives to something they loved more than financial security.

Manet failed exams for a naval commission before he became a "radical" painter. Matisse was a law clerk, Gauguin a stockbroker, and van Gogh a preacher. They moved from "amateur" to the realm of "professional" simply by painting from their hearts and learning how to express what they knew was in them. I'm sure there are those among us who, much like these famous artists, maintain a "day job" and produce wonderful art on their time off.

As I wandered up and down those spiral ramps, reveling in Kandinsky's genius, it brought home the fact that we can all learn and build on everything that has gone before. We are not all geniuses. Most of us won't ever be featured in magazine articles or win major show awards, never have a one-man show or see our work in a museum. But if we examine our reasons for painting, maybe status, money, or skill aren't what attract us. Maybe what we really love is what the creative act gives us all; power to express ourselves beyond the spoken word or physical act. Visual art is an ancient and admired commodity in the societies of mankind. It is powerful and comprehensive in its scope. It is immediate and long lasting in its effect. It is part of us from *Good Night Moon* to Jackson Pollock - from Crayola to glazing effects.

My point is, no matter who you are, no matter your skill level, your most important artistic asset is your love of art. That may translate to any number of reasons for your desire to create, but the reasons may be just a validation of your desire to make art. In short, we don't need to be artists for any reason other than that we want to create art. And we don't need an MFA to become artists.

This is why I constantly remind students that *they* need to make decisions about their work, not ask their teacher, "What do you think I should do?" but ask themselves, "What do I want?" I believe learning to rely on your own instincts and information is good training for the day when you won't have a teacher handy. So I advise: use others' critiques as a primary learning tool, and take to heart only what works for you to make your art better.

Sooner or later we all have to rely on ourselves to do our work. We have to learn to be responsible for it, and to alter, improve, revise, redo, discard, work over, start over or do whatever it takes to get it right. And "right" means what the artist likes best. What you like best.

Drawing On Photographs

A long-time student of mine recently asked me was there anything wrong with copying a photograph. My response was that if it wasn't copying something photographed by someone else, have at it! In fact, even if someone else took the picture, and didn't mind you using it, it was fine. But I thought at the time, *maybe it's time to talk about photos a bit*.

Painting today would not be the same had it not been for the photograph. It showed us how horses and people look in action, it taught us that we could incorporate new visual tools and visual standards into our painting styles (e.g., photorealism), and gave us a valuable tool for taking home the great outdoors or other images we wanted to paint, or *paint from*, in our studios. I've italicized "paint from" because there's always an issue as to whether a *real* artist should project a photo and trace from it.

I think that is a non-issue. David Hockney proposed through the Hockney-Falco thesis (see the book, *Secret Knowledge*) that without the use of projections by the *camera obscura*, Renaissance realism wouldn't and couldn't have happened, and we wouldn't be painting realistic scenes today. Their device didn't catch the image and hold it like our cameras will, but it did project the real world on a canvas or wall so Vermeer and others could draw it and then match the textures, colors and perspective in paint. So what's the difference?

Some say that the ability to draw is central to being a painter, and that to lack that ability is to beg the definition of the word "artist". Others say that it doesn't matter if you can draw, since you can just trace a photo or even just paint over it! Some say it doesn't matter. What do I say?

Well, I'm ok with whichever way you want to do it. I'm currently working on a series of paintings taken directly from old family photos of my parents' generation. I blow them up and trace them. I add color and texture, and try to draw them as accurately as I can. But one reason I do this is that the photos themselves speak to a different time and different generational conventions and interests. I can't express more than that, when that's what intrigues me about them. Other photos I use as a basis for a painting by drawing the scenes they contain. I use my own color and change them as I see fit, because the subject isn't so much an interest as the composition, feeling and design that I make of it. Would I try a photorealistic painting? No. Why? Two reasons: (1) I'm too impatient to do a good job and (2) I find copying very boring.

This is not to belittle those who seek the other path. There are some terrific photo realists at work in watercolor these days, and I love their work when I see it. There's also the current flap in the American Watercolor Society. Its top award this year went to a woman who allegedly copied a stock photo, perfectly allowable under the law if you pay the appropriate fees, which was allegedly not part of her agreement with the stock photo company. In fact, there is some allegation that she really painted over the actual print of the photo. It's all getting hard to deal with isn't it? And if you copy exactly, whose design is it?

I prefer to just find a different statement for my paintings, and I try to inspire that in my students. I don't believe you need to find a photo and copy it precisely to the pixel to have a good piece of art. Neither do you need to use prehistoric charcoal on a cave wall to have a good piece of art. Just use all of these as tools to find your own personal statement about the world. We have more and more ways to do things. Let's try to be experimental in our choices, original in our products, and forgiving in our outlook.

Art: The Fountain of Youth

I know I'm getting older. I can't remember from month to month whether I've sent in my column for this newsletter (hence the reprints). Neither can I recall names. Not just of people I know but seldom see, but also of famous artists whose work I've enjoyed and taught about for years. Neither can I remember some of the lists I need to keep in mind, like the Principles of Design or the Elements of Design or the Characteristics of Color; all stuff I now have to have in a list when I teach, even if I still design and paint as though they were my middle name. I could get depressed by this except for one thing; the artists I know who are older than I don't seem to be making less art or having more difficulty learning about art. But I think I've found the fountain of youth – or at least longer life.

One friend who is 91 is still sharp as a tack, and her work has been equally to the point. Another, who is still learning, is 90, still shows up at workshops, paints outdoors, and generally is the first to bend my ear with questions whenever we're in the same room. And her work is getting substantially better all the time. There are tons of others, from relative youngsters like me to not quite so young like those above, who can - and are - still reveling in art and all it has to offer. I'm beginning to think it can extend your life.

In fact, look at some of the deceased famous artists:

Andrew Wyeth: d. age 91

Salvador Dali: d. age 84

Pablo Picasso: d. age 92

Robert Rauschenberg: d. age 82

Henri Matisse: d. age 85

Michelangelo: d. age 89

Monet: d. age 86

Georgia O'Keefe: d. age 99

Betty H. Austin (my mom): d. age 90

And the list goes on!

Of course I'm looking on the bright side. I haven't listed all those who kicked off early, but let's face it; young artists don't necessarily follow the healthiest lifestyles, do they?

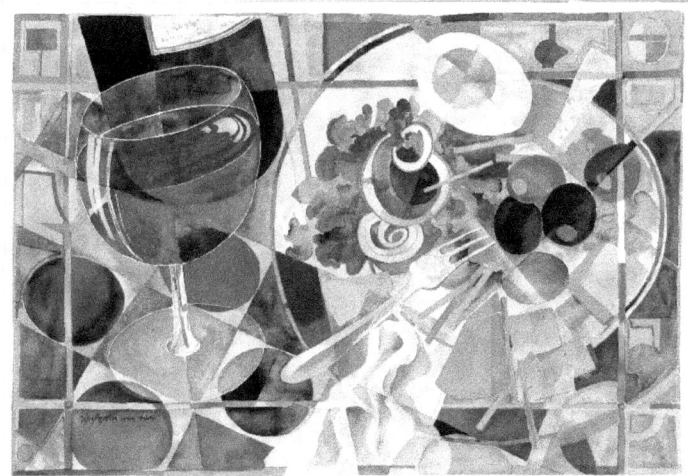

Bistro II

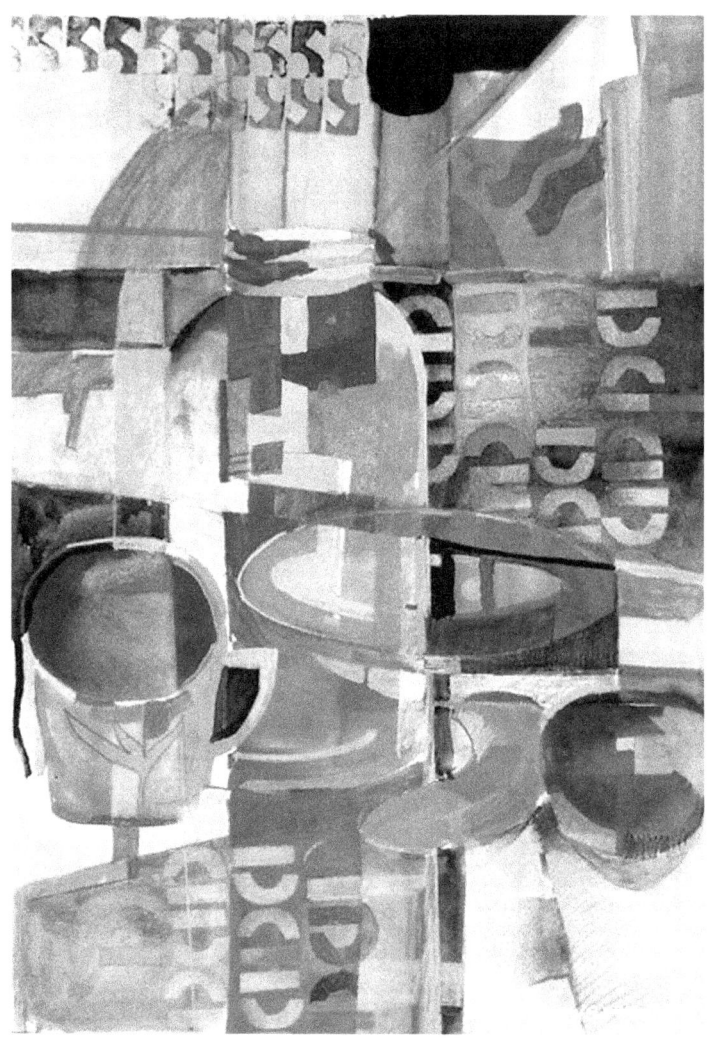

Aunt Fern's Ball Jar

5
CHOICE POINTS

How To Make A Painting

We all make our paintings and think we have to know a lot about art and be careful with color, value and design - and it does help. But, pared down to its basics, the real way to make a painting is simple:

1. Put your brush in some water

2. Mix it with some paint, and

3. Put the paint on the paper

Elementary? *Of course*. A painting is only paint on paper. But we forget this simple fact when we paint. My students often come to me with half-finished paintings which they want to improve, and the only way is to crop drastic sections from their designs.

"Oh, no!" they say, "I just love those *(insert leaves, colors, houses, chicken feathers, etc.)*". Invariably, my reply is that a painting is just paint on paper. It isn't art unless it withstands the scrutiny of viewers, critics and fellow artists. And art isn't about the little parts of the painting that the *artist loves*; it's about the big ideas, concepts and feelings that the artist *imparts* through the painting, using originality and good design. Too much investment in a small part of the painting means the other parts will suffer. The whole needs to be a balanced statement, and you need to be responsible for that balance.

So the next time you step back and review your painting at mid-completion, think about these things:

- What is this painting about?

- Is that the most prominent thing in this painting?

- Is the painting too much about something else?

- Can I change the painting to re-focus on my original idea through redesign, corrections or revisions to the existing painting?

If the answer to the last three is "no," then start over. Remember, it's only paint on paper.

We Are Not Cameras: A Painter's View

I love photography. I took a beginning photography course in college under the great Jerry Uelsmann and learned it was beautiful in the hands of a master, but too technical and labor intensive for me. I still shoot outdoor stuff I might want to paint later. I tried painting from photos without the on-site experience, but it seemed an impossible task.

Getting everything in the photo into the painting was impossible, tedious and boring, and came out looking like a collection of things instead of a painting. At some point, while painting outdoors, I did a thumbnail sketch (tiny but the same proportions as my final painting). I realized that its lack of photographic detail was a good thing. So why not use the thumbnail for basic composition, major shape and rough color selection? I did it and it worked for me - but it took a long while to cope with the lack of detail.

When photography was first publicly available, most people had only seen portraits or landscapes rendered in paint, rare in this country. The popular standard for a painting was how much it looked like the subject. With photos anyone could have a portrait made with an incredibly accurate likeness. They could see and buy the Parthenon in glorious detail, the faces of presidents, murderers, and animals in the wild. Eventually, George Eastman's genius (Kodak) made everyone a photographer ("artist") overnight.

This, in part, is why we want to paint a scene just like we see it, but boggle when we try to paint from a photo. The fact is, our sight (brain) is selective and focuses on what we want/like/hate about things we see – the camera doesn't. It is a machine. It is stupid about art. It only sees in complete detail what's in front of it when you push the button.

Learning to parse, substitute, and invent are as creative as the actual painting you do. This means you are not lying if your barn painting doesn't include the Corvette parked in front. It means you are being creative with the stuff you have to work with.

At a plein air workshop I taught in West Virginia, an elderly lady positioned herself under a tree for shade's sake, with a another small tree between her and the scene, and started painting. The subject, the Seneca Rocks, is a great 900 foot high natural formation of breathtaking beauty. As I walked by later I saw she had painted the tree in front of her, no rocks. When I asked why no rocks, she said, "Because all I can see is this tree in front of me."

When I suggested she just not paint the tree (you could see the rocks through it), she said, "You mean it's ok for me to just NOT paint it? Even though it's there?"

That lady was a victim of photography. So will you be until you learn that the painting you do is up to YOU. It's not what you see before you, but what you put on the paper that's art. Now go paint those rocks!

The 'What to Paint' Blues

I try hard; I really, really do, but you know what? I just can't always seem to find a subject that I want to paint. A good friend who used to paint outdoors with me on Sundays would spend hours looking for a good site with me in the car, and then we'd be down to about an hour to really paint anything.

I'm better than I used to be, though. I keep plenty of travel photos, old family shots, random flower and nature shots, not to mention books of sketches to rely on. I realized a few years back that I really don't have any excuse not to paint. In fact, when I sat down and looked at my work and my whole production process, I discovered I wasn't bored with the subjects, I was bored with my way of painting them.

Now, if Dr. Phil were there, he'd say, "...and how's that workin' for ya?" I figured it wasn't, because I needed a new attitude about the whole thing. So I came up with some things to encourage positive behavior in myself when I grew complacent or grumpy:

• There are lots of people in the world who want more than anything to be able to paint. *Use your gifts.*

• There are always flowers. You must humble yourself before their beauty.

- There's always the interior of your home. See what other artists since Rembrandt and Vermeer have done with so humble a subject.

- Like figures and/or portraits? Ask a painting buddy to pose, and then swap off. Even if your paintings aren't the greatest, you can laugh during the time you're together.

- Try that new technique you read about in *Watercolor Magic*, or just take some of those scraps you've saved and PLAY! You may find a prize-winning technique.

- Got an old photo of an ancestor or loved one in their first Model T? What a subject to get creative with! All old browns or hot, intense complements? Bright lines or soft grays?

You get the idea. It's just as important to find a way to make yourself paint as to actually learn and practice painting. So try these ideas or - make up your own! Aren't you supposed to be the creative type?

Background Checks

Backgrounds aren't always easy because we focus on the stuff that's up close. We also tend to paint that way. But - look around you. If you're indoors there are always rectangles in the background. Try using these for big shapes of color/value and composition. If you're outdoors, try simplifying the shapes you see in the background. Use a shape or shapes you've seen elsewhere to back up the main subject. Adjust the color and value to make the painting sing! Who's going to notice where a palm tree is or isn't? It's only paint and paper, after all.

For great background lessons check out work by Polly Hammett and Charles Reid. One of their secrets is their ability to divide compositions into simple shapes. Backgrounds often play against the subject, e.g., an organic shape (female figure) against geometric shapes (windows or paintings hanging on a wall). This contrast makes it easy to identify the subject, and gives life to the composition by the tension produced between soft and hard shapes.

Outdoors offers similar opportunities. Remember that softening edges and graying colors in distant shapes makes them look further away (atmospheric perspective). If the shapes are trees, you don't need to show every leaf and twig. The big shapes are just fine, and you can make them dark or light, soft or hard edged, organic or geometric, intense or grayed. Skies are the same. Roads, walks, buildings, etc., are all shape potential.

You may want to use the organic/geometric mode outdoors (flowers with a door beyond). The same goes for outdoor and indoor shapes and for compositions in general. Make them big and make them interesting.

For more on shapes, read Ed Whitney on shapes and interlocking, and read Skip Lawrence on shapes and dominance. Check out my "Big Women" series for backgrounds as an active compositional device.

Photo-Ops/Painting-Ops

Photos are great for artists and have been used by them for inspiration and for recording information since photography first came on the scene (Alex Powers lectures on how photography has changed painting). I personally encourage my students to use photos, but as a reference, not as a primary source for painting because *the camera focuses on everything*.

When our eyes see, our minds only focus on maybe a half percent of the available data to avoid confusion. But the camera records it all, down to the smallest detail. Most of us suffer from the childhood urge to copy something slavishly in order to "get it right," so we tend to go overboard with a photograph. It is too easy to obsess on the detail in a photo and forget the real subject your creative right brain saw.

I ask my classes to use an intermediary step such as overlaying the photo with tracing paper to get the big, important shapes and work out the compositions without looking at the original. Then, when the final is laid out to their satisfaction they can peek at the print and use it as a reference for color, or whatever detail they desire.

Even for my abstract work I almost always start from a drawing from life, whether figures, a still life or a landscape. It just helps me to get a feel for the real character of the objects I'll be transforming on my own. I then make snapshots and use them for reference after I've developed a real composition and some value and color studies.

The camera is not only a wonderful tool for recording information, but also for transferring it into the computer for further experimentation in color, composition, and design. The whole issue for me has been "do we want to copy or interpret?" It seems the photography should be left for photographers, but we can always use a tool to help us better express ourselves in art.

Crutches

It has occurred to me that we use crutches. Not the kind you need to walk (I've used those, too), but the kind you depend on to make a painting work...those hackneyed, clichéd, actions you take over and over and over, without thinking or looking closely at the results. What's wrong with that, you might ask?

Well, crutches get in the way of a REAL solution to the problem.

I have a former student who is a good painter, always quick and receptive to new ideas, with a good sense of composition and a great sense of humor. But in the midst of one class exercise, I realized she habitually used an entirely inappropriate color (a dark, olive green) as an outline or shadow color in virtually every painting she did. I pointed out that it brought down the color impact of her work, and she responded, "I didn't even know I was using it. It was just automatic, I guess." She quit using that color by turning her palette around so she couldn't automatically go for it. The quality of her paintings improved 100 percent; she threw away the crutch.

We all develop habits, both in painting and in other parts of our lives. Some are helpful, some detrimental, but since they're habits, we hardly ever think about them. "Bad" painting habits are bad only because they limit our abilities. They are crutches. To avoid them, try to bring "fresh eyes" to every step of what you do.

Ask yourself these questions:

-What is there about this painting that I've done over and over on past work?

-Does it contribute to or detract from the quality I want?

-Is it a habit, or is it part of my painting style?

-If a habit, is it a crutch?

-If it's a crutch, what action would remove it from my painting vocabulary?

Crutches are normally used as a compensation for a disability. If the disability is removed, the crutches should go. The one habit you should always have is to look deep into yourself as you paint, and *keep the creative - get rid of the rote.*

Hot Dates and Cool Heads

There has arisen, due to the inquiry of a prestigious CFWS member (well, aren't they all?) a question as to the propriety of writing a date on one's paintings. I don't know why I should be judge and jury of dating our work, but here's what I have discovered and what I think.

I started out dating each and every piece I painted – good, bad, and indifferent – and I mean everything from sketches to finished pieces. I was convinced that I would soon become a great artist and, like Dean Mitchell, have books written about me, my humble beginnings, and my rise to the top. For the sake of future generations, I would have my work dated so librarians and collectors would know the period and time of any work's creation. Like so many good ideas, this one was based on a false premise: that anyone would really give a hoot about my work, let alone its birthday. So, after several years of this, I began to realize that there were flaws in my plan.

First, who cared? A signature was really all that was needed, along with initials of organizations which verified your ability to be randomly selected as worthy of membership. Second, I began to amass lots of unsold paintings with dates from several years prior. Maybe people didn't like the <u>idea</u> of buying an "old" painting. Maybe they just didn't like old paintings. How would it sound? "I just bought a Ken Austin painting that's seven years old!" And the answer would be, "Why didn't you get a new one? Were the old ones on sale?"

While there is a certain logic to that answer, it isn't one I want associated with my painting. I hope I'm not a "fire sale" kind of guy.

But, secondly, there are some benefits to not dating your work. The first is that you won't get asked why it hasn't sold in seven years. Another is that it doesn't age in other places. For instance, if you've had it in a gallery for five years unsigned and move it to another gallery, no one in the new venue will know how long it's been hanging around (no pun intended).

Another is that if you haven't dated it, and it hasn't been in competitions, who's to know its age? Lots of competitions have a maximum age of two or three years for entry. But if it hasn't been in a competition since its inception, what's the difference? Two years, three years, six years? So enter it anyhow! Not that I would do such a thing, but someone with better sense might. And would it matter? I don't think so, because who would know? And is "younger is better" really a philosophy I agree with?

What matters more? I think records of your paintings are very important. Why? Because if someone steals a painting, or if one is destroyed, or if someone wants you to give a talk or you want to put together a professional bio or a proposal for a solo show, you'll need good photos, dimensions, mediums, titles and (gasp!) dates of creation. If your paintings are sold, you should have the collector's name and the amount. All of this stuff can be important at some time.

It takes a cool head to sit and enter these items for every finished piece you produce, whether for sale, exhibition, or something you just want to keep.

I'm terrible at maintaining records. But I do have the above information for about the last 10 years, even if it's not organized and other, less complete (slides, collectors names, dates) that go back 20 years.

So, if you think dates are hot stuff, sure, put them on your work for all to see. But beware! They can come back to bite you.

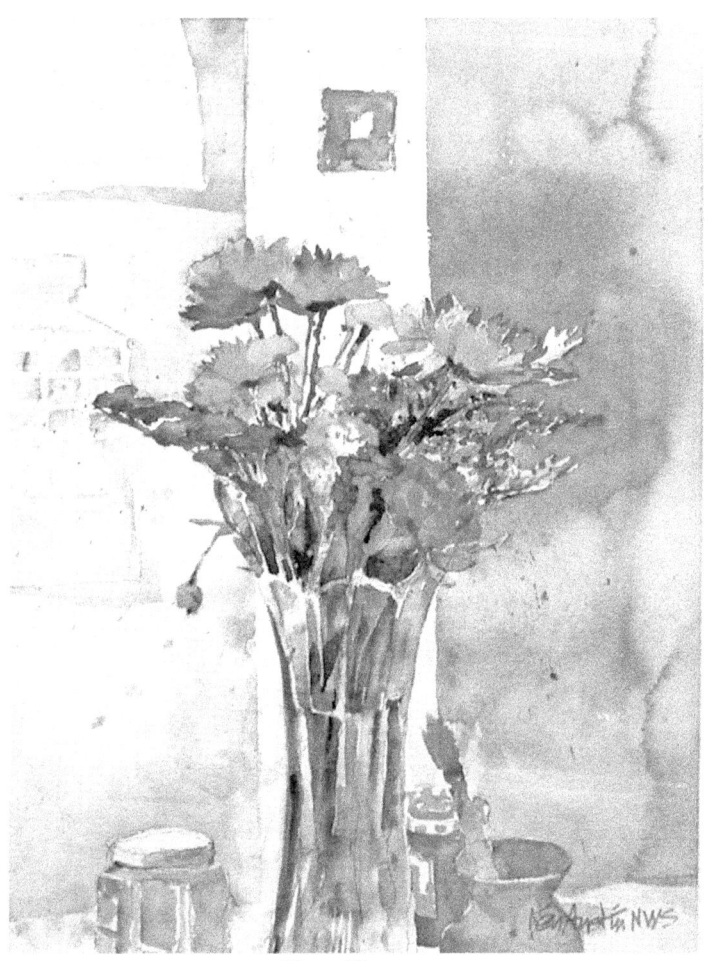

Glass Vase

6
SHOWTIME

To Show Or Not To Show?

Ok, so Shakespeare never entered a competition for watercolor. I have entered many and gone through rejections, acceptances, alternate designations that didn't pan out, won prizes and still lived. So far, anyhow.

I am not a gambler by nature or choice, but there is a certain degree of chance in most shows. Even really good paintings sometimes don't get selected because of the juror's personal taste and opinions on art. So, it's not all up to you. But that poses the question, "What *is* up to you?"

First of all, be sure you cover the basics and do it right:

-Get good slides. Slides should match the original in value and color, and be sharp and clear. No mat or background at all - only black.

-Use the checklist. For most shows the prospectus will have a checklist. Follow it. It has all the steps you need to get your slides, money and forms in proper order.

-Label the slide correctly. Use the right size pen and put all the info required in the prospectus on the slide in the position shown.

-Pay attention to the calendar. More than once, I have submitted a slide of a painting already scheduled to hang in another show and sent the wrong painting to hang. Embarrassing! You must also be alert to the deadlines for returning your painting if it's selected.

-Submit your best. How do you know? Well, if you don't know, you're in trouble. And even if you might know, the juror might not agree with you. You often get to send two or three, so send the best two or three you have!

Second, choose your shows: If you're just starting, local shows are great to get the feel of showing. Regional shows are more challenging.

Finally, learn to handle rejection: If you didn't learn this as a teenager, now's your chance. You might get lots of rejection notices but eventually you'll be accepted.

So keep your head and hopes high and someday that call will come, "I'm pleased to tell you that you've been awarded..."

Austin's Theory of the Artist's Challenge

This isn't a big, involved theory on aesthetics or the meaning of art. This is one way to think about how your work gets looked at, wanted, and bought.

I teach in my workshops that there are three significant stages in the viewer's relationship to paintings. Each of these is within the artist's control, but to different degrees. They are:

1. *Engagement:* When a viewer looks at your work, does he or she spend only a few seconds and move on to the next one? If so, you need to learn how to make your work engage the viewer. The old quote, "First impressions are everything," is apt in art. In short if you can't get them to look at your painting, they won't get to the second stage. (The artist has 90% control over this stage – think of painting a red bullseye; 'nuff said?)

2. *Involvement:* Involvement is the second, the "hook" stage, where the viewers should find something unique to your style or subject, something more interesting, and something with which they can identify. Viewers will often seek a reason to like a painting, and so the detail, technique, or feeling of the painting is effective enough to involve them in your statement. (The artist has about 60% control over this stage.)

3. *Commitment:* Beyond engagement and involvement, the artist's work is pretty much helpless in cementing a

relationship with a viewer. This third stage is up to your viewers, since there must be sufficient reason in their minds to make them want to own the painting. If they love kitties and you painted rectangles, your best work can't make them like your painting enough to hang it on their wall. How many times have you heard, "I really liked that painting but, ..."? You can fill in the blanks. (Sorry, only maybe 2% on this one. You can't please everyone all the time.)

So what can you do about it? You can analyze your work to see if it meets the criteria for each stage. You can check other artists' work from this standpoint and deduce their techniques for dealing with the first two stages. If you speak with them on this subject, they likely won't answer questions about these three stages, because - well, they're artists and they just paint the way that feels best, the way that says what they want to say. But you might have just as much to say in your art, and just need some techniques that can help you understand how to get people's attention without sacrificing your individual style and taste.

While this is, in my opinion, the way people engage with art, there is no gauge as to which individual actually goes through all of these steps and to what degree. Remember, some people buy for color, some for décor, and some for investment. So this is only my guess (okay, so I lied about the 'theory' stuff) at what makes someone look at your paintings. But it's an informed guess, based on 25 years with galleries and more than too many openings without sales, where I watched what happened as people started really looking at paintings, and who chose, who moved on, who inspected, and who was there for the free wine and hors d'oeuvres (a surprising number, by the way).

Nonetheless, it's a good thing to think of the above (no, the theory, not the hors d'oeuvres) as you paint, and see how they enrich your work. Get the big, blocky stuff arranged and then work to connect, disconnect, direct, color, texture and create shapes and lines from that surface. This process is pretty common to watercolor artists, but if you think of it as a series of three fairly separate exercises during the design of your painting, you can have fun with them and improve your paintings simultaneously.

If all this seems too heady for you right now, maybe you need to get deeper into watercolor and increase your knowledge of technique and design.

Showing Your True (Water) Colors

In 1977 I joined the Watercolor Art Society, Houston (WAS-H) and entered a membership show. It was three years before my work was hung in a membership show, another two before it was accepted into a national show. Over the last three years I've been in 13 national shows. I've been rejected enough over the years to realize that this isn't really a random process.

Here are some tips for those of you who like to compete:

1. Study the competition - try to discern why *they* get in but *you* don't.

2. Learn about the sponsoring society and their previous shows. For instance, do they like traditional or experimental work? How many entered and how many were selected?

3. Get advice - while looking at selected paintings, ask an expert if your work stacks up, why not, and what to do.

4. Know the jurors' work - jurors have opinions and biases about the *kind* of work they select. I feel most juror/abstract painters also appreciate representational painting. They come from that background. The reverse ain't necessarily so.

5. Your slide must make an impression in five seconds. Jurors must rip through 500 to 1300 slides to select 100. Traditional advice (which works often but not always) is to paint with *strong* contrast, *clear* design, and *good* craftsmanship.

6. Photography counts. If you aren't a photography professional then pay one to make your slide. It only costs a few bucks.

7. Jurors are independent thinkers - jurors who are friends of mine or those whose work I like don't always choose my paintings, and if they do, don't always give me prizes.

8. Be ready for the thrill of victory, or the agony of rejection - remember, you *are going to lose* some of the time. It only means that someone didn't select your work, not that you (or they) are bad.

Conclusion - do what you love best. Learn, paint, practice, paint. Keep painting. Keep trying.

The Jury Is Ouch!

You know the feeling if you've ever competed. You agonize over your best work, deciding which pieces to submit. You carefully photograph it, get it on a disk and send it in, with visions of being in a show with others whose work you admire – maybe winning an award! Maybe getting accolades as you accept the Best of Show! Maybe ...Well, who knows what?

I've written before that if you enter, you should check out other shows the juror has juried, in order to learn something of his/her tastes in art. Don't paint to meet those tastes (you probably won't be doing your best if you do), but seeing those other shows may help you to understand the breadth and depth of the juror's tastes. You will see that some artists win, no matter what their style, and that they're the ones who almost always win big. Discount these. Their work is so "good" it transcends personal preferences, and all jurors will choose their work for just that reason. Focus on what the rest of the work looks like. See if you can ferret out the juror's likes. You never see the "also entered" paintings unless you go to the reviews which some societies ask the juror to give. It's revealing when they speak about their personal likes and dislikes, and what they look for in paintings.

Having been a juror for several shows over the past few years, both watercolor and all-media, I thought it might be a good thing to talk about my parameters for "good" work. Please note that these might change with the date, weather, my tastes, or other things we can't control. Also, please note that I have a right to change my mind at any time.

I like to see the best of something and/or a different take. When something is painted better than anything else, it's a snap to select. But it's easy for artists to get in a rut, and the pictorial results can be boring, especially if your subject is the same one as dozens of other entries. That's why judging in Florida, for instance, can warp your attitude toward lily pads, birds of paradise and palm tree close-ups. It makes it hard to be fair to a painting if the subject has been done over and over and over. But if I'm intrigued seeing one of these subjects done well *in a different way*, far enough from the norm to be interesting, I'm going to like the *idea* of it as much as the actual painting. I also like to see some craftsmanship. Having a good idea doesn't count if the artist doesn't know the medium, or can't get the paint on right. Making roses that look cut from steel won't get kudos from me. And I love good composition – color, shape, balance, et al. – but it still has to be *about something*. If it's a photo-likeness and that's all, what's to like? But if it's a photo-likeness with a whole new point of view, well, it's going a lot further.

Beyond that, I love color, and I often see mediocre paintings that could be great if the artist had just put enough color in them. It's hard to appreciate a sunset when it's weak and gray. White, pale babies just don't make my heart go pit-a-pat, and Davy's Gray flowers look like a zombie bouquet.

Finally, I look for good drawing, balance, and feeling. Does the painter care about the subject, or is she just a camera? Does it speak to us or is it waiting for us to speak to it? Does it shout at us or does it whisper? Does it involve us emotionally, does it bore us to tears, or is it just tawdry banality?

These are some things for you to think about as you decide which of your masterpieces to send off to a juried show. (But only if I'm going to jury the show - something not likely to happen for a long time.) Nonetheless, thinking about what you paint as you paint is an essential part of the process. And, as I often tell my students:

"Follow your heart, but let your mind guide!"

What, Me Copy?

Our local Watercolor Society recently decided we should not accept paintings into shows if they are painted in a classroom or workshop situation. Such issues are bound to surface as we guide our society into its second decade. A natural part of growth, these discussions and their resolution clear the air, force clarity, and maintain structure.

The logic for excluding such paintings is that accepting them gives an unfair advantage over competitors who didn't get an instructor's help on their paintings and/or that artists should only submit completely original work.

Not all classes are alike. Some classes inspire students to paint in new, exciting ways. Some classes instruct students to paint in specific (occasionally exciting) ways. Sometimes teachers paint on their students' work as I do (only with their permission).

Occasionally that painting is better than anyone ever thought it would be. And while it may be, the student's painting it isn't all theirs. Would you break the rule to show it? I wouldn't. The rule says "no". And entering classwork sure isn't fair to those entrants who sweat it out on their own, some because they can't afford a workshop or can't schedule for classes, or maybe because they want the painting to be all their own original work!

The rule is certainly not rare or divisive. I have checked the show prospectuses for five nationally renowned watercolor shows, (the American, National,

Florida, and Philadelphia Watercolor Societies, and Watercolor Art Society – Houston). Three specify no classroom or workshop work, the other two stress "only original work." Sure, some classwork slips by, but it's the rare exception. The fact is we all have to draw the line somewhere. The Florida Watercolor Society says it's ok to enter paintings done outside class, but critiqued by a teacher, then redone and re-critiqued as many times as you wish. Or, submitting your own copy of work you did in class isn't unlawful. But any work painted in a classroom is NOT allowed. Why? Like I said, you have to draw the line, and that's where they've drawn it. It's also where our board has drawn it.

We can't expect jurors to know what has been painted in class and what hasn't. Purposely not following this rule would be cheating your friends and fellow artists. That's not a good thing. In fact, it's infantile and wrongheaded. And I know you are all above that.

On With the Show

It takes a lot to put a painting out where the public can admire, ridicule or (worse) disregard it. I've had all three things happen to mine in shows, big and small, good and bad. The comments can be hard, but it's always good to try for some recognition.

There are lots of reasons why people enter shows; some folks are VERY competitive; others want to win recognition; some want it on their checklist of accomplishments so they will be credible as artists, teachers, or leaders in their field.

I've probably entered shows for all of those reasons at one time or another, but this time I found myself entering for one reason only; to show support through participation. This may come as a shock, but you don't ever, ever HAVE to enter competitive shows. They are difficult, bruising affairs if you aren't accepted, and if you are, you wonder if you'll make the next one, and the next, etc. Our local show is easier than most, since we just had to show up on time, meet the requirements and pay our bucks.

I really like that, and I think Central Florida Watercolor Society (CFWS) was wise to approach juried shows in a careful and supportive way for our membership. I expect our member shows to become more selective and exclusive sometime in the future, and I also expect we will see some shows open to nonmembers. Both will be juried for inclusion and for awards, and some people will be just like the woman at our table at the Florida Watercolor Society (FWS) awards banquet in Sarasota this year, devastated because her teacher had told her if she entered her painting in the show she was sure to get an award. Well, she wasn't accepted into the FWS show and she was tortured by the disappointment, ready to talk with an attorney.

This is not a healthy way to show your interest and support for watercolor painting. If you enter a competition, you should get ready to be disappointed. A lot of us have been. It's the rare few who never fail at competitions, so we have to be able to blow it off. Understand, especially in a membership show, that entry is an indication of your support. A prize-winning juggernaut's struggle starts here, but at our society level, the honor is in supporting a group of people dedicated to a visual art form that is beautiful, difficult, addicting and as meaningful as any of the many other ways we have of contributing to our everyday enjoyment of life. And I'd say that kind of honor is really a good thing.

Thoughts on Presentation

This bit of science, intuition and experience is intended to help you know what to do with your work after you finish painting it, and before you enter it in a show/put it in a gallery/show it to your mom, whatever. In other words, how it *needs* to look. Do you need a mat? How do you select a color? A frame?

For any painting to be framed appropriately, there are two issues to resolve: purpose and place. Are you putting it in a gallery, a competition, or in someone's home?

The main purposes for matting are:

-Showing or selling (depends on standards of gallery, sale venue, etc.)

-Competition (standards usually stated-no exceptions)

-Hanging in home or work area (depends on surrounding, style of decor, colors)

Professional craftsmanship in matting/framing is always better, unless you have lots of experience and the right equipment.

Taste is up to you or your client's representative. Better to err on the conservative side.

Matting is often done with a computer-operated machine, so cutting different size sides, all same size, or whatever, is no penalty to you. If your order is small, ask what kind of partials they have left, and see if you can get a discount. Mat material comes in all colors, various levels of archival quality, and some with special effects (such as a core that's a different color from the mat).

Remember when your art is going in a home or business environment, it's not *your* wall. Though the painting is your baby, to decorators, architects, owners, and owners' families it may just be another piece of decor. Well...they DID pay for it!

If a buyer asks how to reframe it, remember, free advice is time from your busy schedule, and a possible road to a bad relationship. Be prepared with your decorator's or framer's card and write your name on the back so they know you're helping their business. Tell the buyer they'll do a good job, but to give them your card. Ask if they want the frame you've put on the painting, and if not, offer to remove it if you can keep it.

Framing can be a hidden cost to the artist. The last gallery I was with wanted my work in "better" frames – code for heavier, more ornate. I said "No", because when a gallery takes its cut, they take it for the frame too. Framing and matting are an out-of-pocket cost to you for which they get 40% or whatever their fee is. You're out the total cost as opposed to your materials ($20?) and time. So if you have a $500 painting with a $200 frame, you have to ask around $900 to get back your frame cost - hard to make a sale that way!

For *your own* matting or framing, be sure your instructions are clear. Write them down, keep a copy if need be and check the finished work every time. Framing is a hectic and demanding business, and errors can be devastating, especially if there's a tight deadline.

As to my own work, I use fairly thin frames, partly because they cost less, but also because I want the work to be the main visual part of the ensemble. I like a nice mat, but I don't use anything but white. I often have mats doubled to give a step-down into the painting. I leave issues of framing and matting for décor to the framer or, more often to the owner's decorator/designer. A good interiors person can pull together a great ensemble for a painting. I recently sold a painting that the designer had framed floated in glass. What a knockout!

Remember, shows and competitions have rules for framing and matting, and they're serious about them! Also remember, if you don't have strict restrictions, a rich or exuberant mat and frame can take attention away from a watercolor painting. You'll only be defeating yourself. If you've done a painting you *think* you'll enter in a competition, but don't know <u>which</u> competition, go conservative and use the strictest limitations to mat and frame. Many shows limit maximum sizes to 40" framed. So if you use a 22" x 30" (full sheet) paper vertically, you'll probably have an inch of total coverage vertical and horizontal, leaving a maximum of 5 ½ inches top and bottom for frame and mat. Not a lot for a painting that size, but still presentable when thoughtfully done.

This advice is based on personal experience. I hope it's not too confusing. I know with a little care and concern your paintings will be even *more* beautiful when they're matted and framed.

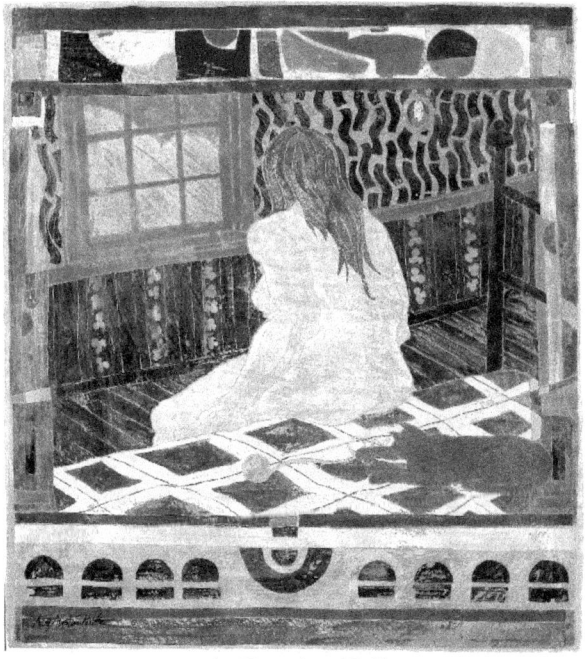

As Evening Falls

Spread the Joy

I was MOST positively impressed by the news from a November watercolor society meeting that we were to bring our paintings to the annual Holiday Meeting, where prizes for paintings wouldn't be offered. In the past this meeting has featured a mini-show wherein the attendees vote on the paintings they like best. Those with the most votes in the various categories (usually by skill levels – beginners, intermediate, etc.) are awarded prizes. Pretty nice prizes too, I might add.

Now, you might wonder why I think the cessation of prizes is a good thing, especially since I seem to have won more than my share of them. Well, that's the reason. If a few people keep winning the prizes, where's the joy of others showing their paintings? Let's face it, fair's fair. In my opinion, we are constantly (and this is good) encouraging our members to participate by working, serving, etc. But this show will encourage members to participate with their art regardless of whether they sit on the board, come to the meetings, or just pay dues.

We've had great workshops, demos and lectures, and we've had terrific fun with all of our other meetings. And I realize that not everyone who paints is ready for someone to judge their work. I do believe, however, if you've painted only for yourself, it's good to begin the arduous task of showing your work to the world. The *world* may or may not agree with you on its content, or aesthetic value, and it may hurt to hear what the *world* says and thinks about your work. But that's the exact value of showing it to your fellow members. *Because every single one of them knows exactly how you feel.* Every one of them at some point either found the courage to show, or didn't. If they did, they know how you're feeling. If they didn't they'll know you're braver than they were. And maybe you'll be the role model they're looking for. Best of all, they'll be forgiving! They know how difficult and precious these creations are to you.

So, why make it a contest? This group of people is bound by a common love for paint and paper. Who among them would want to exclude others from showing their work because of the intimidation of being judged? Not one, I'd say. Certainly not me. Certainly not you. And who else really counts?

Besides that, we will have our share of juried competitions in the coming year. And I can gripe that I didn't win another award because all these new people are showing. And it's all my own fault for writing this column.

Hey, wait a minute. Let me start over!

Final Check

Did you ever start out the door to an event, and think, "I'd better take a final look in the mirror." And then find there's broccoli in your teeth or no belt in your pants or you forgot to brush your hair or put on socks? Well, it's a good idea to do a final check on your paintings too.

We all look at the paintings we do for days or weeks as we paint them, but when we finish we might still be overlooking minor imperfections or correctable items which can make or break a painting in terms of its appeal. Learn to take a few minutes and look at your work. Here are some helpful methods:

Use a mirror - Yep, don't forget it's backwards from what you normally see, so some gaps and surprises might show up pretty quickly. We tend to "read" a painting from left to right, (cultures whose script moves from right to left read paintings in that direction) so the reflection can be a shock.

Use a diminishing glass - This little beauty is the opposite of a magnifying glass; it makes things smaller, still maintaining detail, so it's easier to see the overall design structure. They can be bought from Jerry's Artarama and other art supply houses.

Squint your eyes - It's the old fashioned way to check values and big shapes, or, use a red plastic film to cover the painting, reducing the color contrast, allowing you to see value only.

Use a value gauge - If you see value problems, check with a value gauge to ascertain true value relationships, or take a digital photo and change it to black and white with your computer graphics program.

Use a mat - Most everyone who works professionally uses mat board "L's" to check for final presentation. You never know what the viewers will see until you see it through their eyes, and this little item will keep you from making big mistakes.

Get a fresh view - Put the painting away for a few days or weeks and then bring it out, set it up vertically, with a mat, and look at it in a normal environment. If it's still a winner, get ready to sell it - that check from a buyer is the most satisfying "final check"!

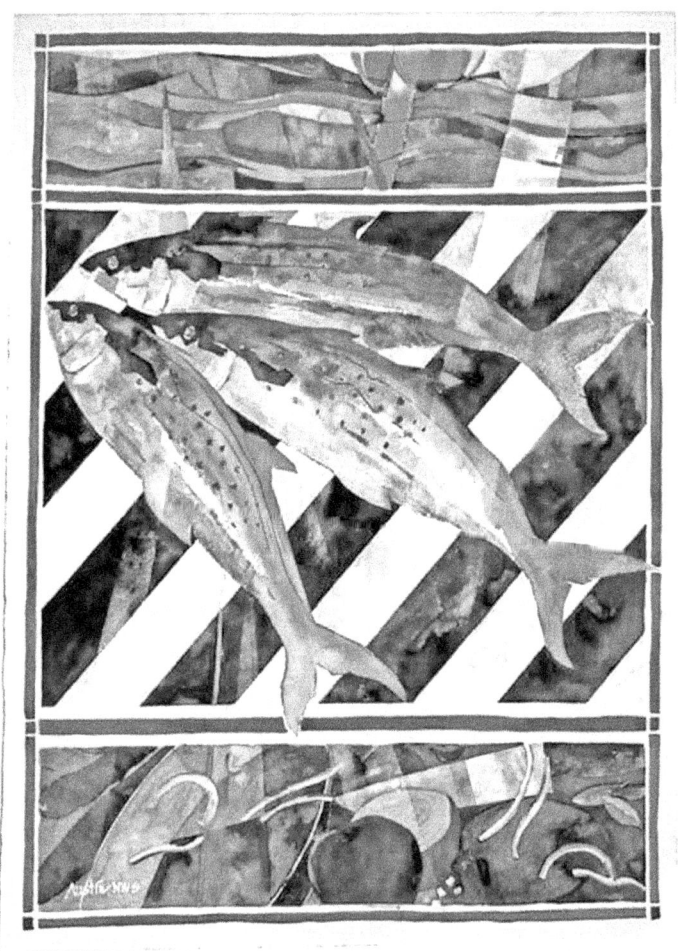

Wholly Mackerel

7
COLORMAKING

Pay Yourself a Complement

Are you a natural at color? Or are you, like me, slightly challenged by it all?

Contrast is an important tool for every painter. We can control the degree of color contrast by their selection and placement.

Color study can increase your painting power because your choice of a color scheme helps you to control the viewer's choices of what to look at, the tension of the painting, and the overall character of your work.

The two most common options for color schemes are complementary and analogous. A complementary scheme (colors across the color wheel from each other) lends tension to a painting because the colors appear more intense against each other (they contrast more), and may "fight" each other. Analogous schemes (colors adjacent on the color wheel) provide a release from tension, and are more peaceful to the viewer. You can have immense control over the appearance and content of your painting, because you can control contrast through color with intensity, value and hue.

Look in art books for paintings by post-impressionists, especially Paul Gauguin and Vincent van Gogh, as well as 20th Century illustrators N.C. Wyeth and Maxfield Parrish. Many of these artistic giants' paintings are studies in the use of complementary schemes to the greatest benefit.

Considerations:

Using color well is a matter of taste and skill. Taste and skill develop over time, and only through practice. There are some things to be aware of:

-If you happen to end up with equal size shapes of complementary colors distributed throughout the composition, they will visually cancel out the normal tension and make the painting appear gray.

-Warm colors will often dominate, whether larger or smaller shapes in your painting. Like real estate, color depends on three things; location, location, location.

-Learn to use colors for emotional value - intense warms excite, blues and greens relax, complements create tension, etc.

- Start with the lines, shapes, composition and value of the painting and deduce the color from it, or vice versa, but always try to be *aware* of what you're doing to the overall statement you're making.

Something of Value

Ok, do you remember the four defining visual characteristics of color? Well, try these: HUE (the color itself, i.e., violet, red, etc.), INTENSITY (often called saturation), TEMPERATURE (is it a warm blue or cool one?), and (get ready for this!) VALUE!

Three-dimensional sight separates same color shapes by their depth, which we can't do on watercolor paper - it's flat. In painting, shapes are the flat divisions of the paper which form a composition. If our eyes can't separate them, we don't know which shape is important and which isn't. No composition. We can use any or all of the above color characteristics to separate shapes visually in painting. Value is the most basic characteristic and easiest to perceive. Why?

Our eyes are built to be sensitive primarily to dark and light. The retina has receptors called rods and cones. Rods perceive darkness and light, and cones perceive color. There are 120 million rods and 6 million cones. It doesn't take an eye surgeon to figure why we're more sensitive to light and dark (value) than to color!

In the natural world, light and dark seldom come in black/gray/white, but as a characteristic of color... dark trees, light skies, even glowing streetlamps all have an element of color (hue) to them. So if you paint with value as a main element (it's ok, so does Andy Wyeth), you should be sure to do value studies (that means black, gray, and white) to help see the shapes and their arrangement (composition). You also should try relying on the other characteristics for your painting style, just to see how it feels. Some well-known watercolor painters with distinctive color-definition styles include: Dan Burt (Hue), Polly Hammett (Value), Stephen Quiller (Temperature), and Frank Francese (Intensity).

Try some of these approaches to see if you are comfortable or entranced with the results. You may get a new lease on watercolor!

It's Just My Impression

I just finished teaching a workshop for the Vero Beach Museum of Art called "Learning from Impressionism", and in order to teach I had to be the one who learned more than anyone else. The thing is, that since that workshop I've become more interested than I ever was in Impressionism and the artists themselves, and have continued my studies of them. I've read articles and checked out library DVD's about them, their work, families, social status, lives and deaths - entertaining and helpful to the struggling watercolor painter (myself included).

One of the more interesting things is how they all relied on contrast to make their paintings lively and arresting to the viewer. The contrast was often carried by the use of black (yep, looks like straight from the tube) and intense complementary colors-particularly that old saw, turquoise and orange. Of course this was new and radical when they started in the 1860's but it brought a new feeling to paintings which involved the viewers directly from first glance.

Not normally a black-out-of-the-tube user, I do mix blacks. My reason for not using tube blacks in watercolor is that it's difficult to grade from black into another color in watercolor without creating a nasty grayed-out sort of transition. This doesn't happen in oils because the paint itself maintains its independent color and can transition with color impact as well as value impact. But when I want a really sharp contrast (dark/light) and a black to color transition I mix the color as thick as I can and simply charge it into the damp black, letting it mix itself.

High contrast in color and value make for lots of prize-winning paintings in shows. Look at Manet (actually a pre-impressionist), Monet, and the others. You'll see a whole new world open before you. And check out some books and DVD's to absorb their theories and final works. These guys and gals were terrific painters, and real leaders for a whole new, redefined concept of art. They changed the way we all see art, and that's only one reason to love their work. Another is it's beautiful.

Clean Colors and Creative Mud

Q: *"How do I get clean colors like I see in books and magazines, especially when I'm trying to create really dark values?"*

Try really deep, strong staining colors like Pthalo Blue and Viridian Green, or Pthalo Green and Quinacridone Violet. Darks mixed from complements are often muddy because they have at least one pigment that is an opaque. The same is true for light and mid value colors - if you mix them on your palette you need to remember three things:

-A dirty palette will make for dirty colors. Keep your palette clean by wiping with a tissue frequently, even if you think you'll need exactly that same color later. Believe me, you won't.

-Mixing complements can produce beautiful grays, but NOT if you mix opaque and transparent pigments. For complement grays use only non-opaque pigments, and the colors will be clear.

-For the best intensity and brightness, try only mixing color on the paper. Use the pure pigment with as little water as possible, and allow it to mix itself on the paper. You'll be amazed at what it does without your interference!

Q: "I love pastel colors, but they get lost in my paintings. How can they be made to stand out more and become a feature?"

Try the old "mud and magic" trick. Pastel colors (light value intense pigments) will stand out best when the background (surrounding) is a mid-value gray. The contrast is even more noticeable when the mid value gray is "muddy", meaning a warm gray, usually in the brown or warm yellow range. Try to simplify your painting into two main color groups - the "mud" and the pastels. Also use pigments which are the colors you want so they will be pure (see above), not mixed on the palette.

Color Mixing

You always hear (from me, anyhow,) "Let the color mix on the paper!", and this is sage advice, because it enlivens the color and makes for spontaneity in your work. But it's not as straightforward as you might think. Because, if you let it mix without controlling the mixing process, it may end up muddy or flawed (with blossoms, or hard edges, or those weird little fingers you get sometimes). So, here are some ways to get color mixes to behave.

1. To add color (whether different or the same) over an existing painted area, the existing area must be wet or dry, not in between. If you want to add a new color and leave part of the existing color the same, you can apply it wet on a dry surface, and blend it from the new to the existing color by rinsing your brush and running a line of clear water at the blending edge of the new color. The new color will weaken in the line of clear water, and blend.

If the existing area is wet, blend by adding the new color *at the same degree of wetness or a little dryer.* Too dry and it will leave a hard edge; too wet and it will puddle and make a mess of the existing color.

2. Try to let color move within a certain shape by adding different colors as you paint. You can add reds to green foliage and violets to blue skies and get a livelier effect than if they are straight out of the tube, or premixed on your palette, but the secret is, *don't over-*

mix them on the paper. By letting them mix themselves, they sing their own songs, and your paintings will gain a new level of interest and activity.

3. Think about what you want the painting to do, color-wise, and follow that idea throughout. Do you want excitement? Stick with complements, quick changes and intensity. Do you want calm? That would be analogous with low value changes and slow color change.

Before you start, experiment with color mixing by trying some small scale mixes. Let the colors do the work by blending into each other and by using your wet line technique to introduce them to each other. Remember to vary the degree of wetness.
Practice makes *almost* perfect. The rest is creativity.

Ken Austin

Muckraking and Colormaking

I just finished teaching a great workshop with a wonderful group of students who wouldn't let me get away with anything. I like that, since all teachers have a tendency to grandstand or BS when they don't really know what they're teaching. I am, of course, above such shenanigans, but nonetheless, I've thought more about the most common issues in watercolor. And a major issue is good color.

This article is devoted to all of us who buy, mix and apply those wonderful colors and still end up with a muddy, mucky, yucky painting. Why do we do this? How are we inferior to other artists? Why aren't our paints acting like Frank Webb's or Steve Roger's? Why aren't our skies bright songs and our shadows dark jewels?

There are four basic parts to color success: the Pigments on your palette (P), their Application to the paper (A), Mixing them together (M), and Positioning for effect (P). Remember that to make color correctly you have to "PAMP"er your painting.

Here are some ideas:

PIGMENTS are available that are brilliant and versatile. Find someone whose painting colors you like and buy the same pigments they use in their paintings.

APPLY the paint as wet or dry as you need it, but with enough fresh pigment to make it count. Try a painting done in full pigment of each of your colors (no mixing!), as much as the brush can hold, only enough water to flow. You'll soon see how much color you've been missing.

MIX colors to make sure your darks are colors. Pthalo Blue or Green and Alizarin Crimson are difficult, staining colors, but they can mix with burnt sienna, oranges, purples, etc. to produce dark greens, blues, or warm or cool blacks. Mixing in Payne's Gray will make gray (duh!) and mixing black with color will make mud almost inevitable. Mix other colors *minimally* on your palette, and let them mix themselves on paper. Place them wet and saturated for best effect.

POSITION your colors for the best effect. Use saturated (intense) colors for attention, soft colors for calm areas. Place colors next to complements for tension, next to analogs for calm. Add small pieces of the major colors in your painting around to provide continuity. Use the bright ones for accents. You can make pure brights look brighter next to grays (especially complementary grays)

Other helpful hints:

-Always use fresh-squeezed pigment. When it begins to dry on your palette, add a thin paint layer on top to soften the existing pigment, and when you're finished for the day, spritz with water.

-Mud can be visually helpful if it's used adjacent to or surrounding an intense color, and if it makes sense in the overall painting design.

-Use tube blacks if you want a pure black in your painting with no variation and overtones of other colors. Otherwise mix your darks, since you can vary those by addition or subtraction of color.

-If you must grade from tube black into another color, apply the color at its deepest value at the edge of the black and then grade toward your desired color intensity or value from there.

-Design and maintain a dominance of color by hue, value, intensity and/or temperature for the painting to really come alive.

-Vary colors *within each* shape. Move from dark to light, light to dark (gradation) or from one color to another, letting them mingle on the paper with little or no brushing.

-Repeat the brightest, most saturated colors in your painting by spotting accents of them for balance in other areas of your design. Sometimes the unexpected, unobtrusive accent is joyful to the eye.

There are some excellent books out there on color by watercolor artists. *Making Color Sing*, by Jeanne Dobie is a great one, as are books by Frank Webb, Nita Leland and Christopher Schink.

Workshops are another good opportunity to learn the ropes, as well as by closely observing the painting techniques of artists whose color work you like. Last but not least is learning by working with friends or in group painting sessions. All of these are wonderful opportunities for you to get into the color...and get your mind (and your paintings) out of the muck!

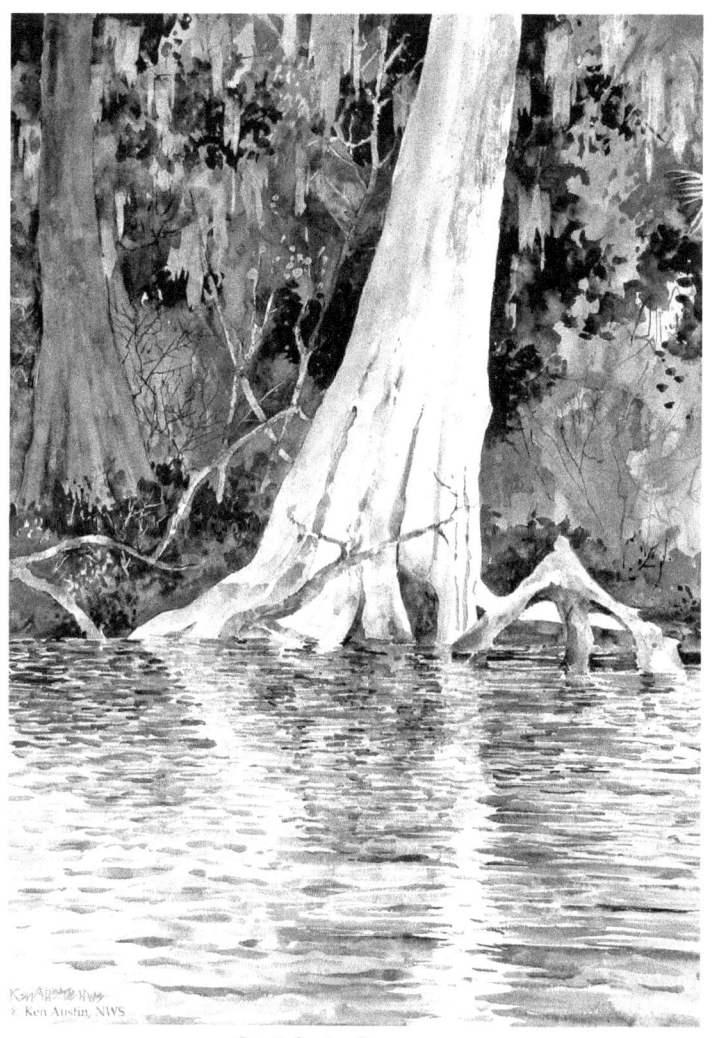

St. John's Cypress

8
PERSPECTIVES ON PAINTING AND COMPOSITION

How to Paint a Painting

For a lot of us, the issue isn't what to paint or when to paint, but where do you start? More importantly, what's next? I've even had advanced students who complained that they didn't really know what to do once started, or where to go next. There's not a given formula for this, but once you have that spellbinding idea you want to pursue (that part's up to <u>you</u> alone!), there is a logic to how to go about the business of making a painting.

This logic comes from the great Skip Lawrence, who is one of my favorite teachers, an especially gifted artist, and an overall great guy.

His steps are (generally):

1. Divide the sheet into shapes.
-Then find a basic compositional concept

2. Define the shapes.
- Make shapes interesting (active or passive)
- Group shapes to create dominance
- Vary them by size and outline

3. Define the composition by contrast, especially:
- Value
- Hue
- Intensity

4. Develop a dominance of statements.
- Group shapes with a similarity
- Vary them by value, form, color, pattern, line, etc. but they must be visually united at some point into dominant and recessive statements

    Heady stuff? Yes. How do you do all these things? The method varies with the artist. Too general? Well, you have to be general when you talk about how to do art, or it'll come back to bite you.

    What's presented here is an outline that suits most painting styles and subject matter, not to mention various artistic temperaments. So, yes, general it is. You'll have to learn how to paint what you want on your own, but I believe you can use this framework to evaluate and progress through the process.

Perspectives on Painting

Does perspective give you the shivers? I've had an architect's education, which requires (or used to, anyhow) a clear knowledge of *linear* perspective (you know, the kind where the railroad tracks converge at the horizon). But there are two distinct types of painters; those who paint for the visual effect of realism (verisimilitude) and those whose lack of linear perspective is a tool for focusing attention on the *abstract qualities* of a painting rather than the *objects* described therein.

Linear perspective, a Renaissance invention, has been around for 1/40th of the history of art. But you may want to take a look at how Cezanne, Matisse, Gauguin, and other painters *disregarded* it in order to achieve specific effects such as tension, or a kind of naiveté in their works. The 19th Century, when this was first done, was a fertile one for art, and really provided the roots for modern and abstract art. Many of the expressionist paintings use non- or naive perspective for effect. All of those artists knew how to use linear perspective, realistic color, classical figure drawing, etc. but all of them still used other means of painting in order to enrich the design of their work, and control the viewer's response to it.

So using "bad" perspective isn't an excuse to do a nice painting of beautiful palms, all in perfect realistic harmony, but with houses whose roofs seem tilted by a small earthquake ("Well, van Gogh did it!"). Ah, yes, but he did it for a reason and with purpose, and his paintings show that.

When bluegrass musicians make a bad chord, they say, "Hey! It's jazz!" Well, it's not jazz, it's a joke to cover their mistakes. And whether you are dedicated to modern statements or traditional ones in watercolor, you have to know how to make things hang together. Otherwise they may never hang at all: at least not in galleries or shows.

The Line Starts Here

We all started with lines. We did little squares with triangles on top, added a circle above and made some "v-birds". THEN we came back and filled in the blue sky, the yellow sun and the red brick house and asked the teacher to look at it. And you know what? We still do. We outline our subjects and then paint them in. Then we erase the lines (well, not me, but then I'm lazy and I like them for the surface interest they add).

But this is about lines as a subject or a major element of your painting. In fact, line is one of the elements of design, so maybe we should explore it more. How do I love line? Let me count the ways:

1. Let those lines show. Make them an expressive part of your statement. (Toulouse Lautrec, Vincent van Gogh)

2. Let them show as a repetitive, rhythmic part of the expression of your composition. (Ed Whitney)

3. Let them tell the viewer what's close and what's farther away by using heavy lines for the closer profile, and lighter for the farther. (Moira Huntley)

4. Get intense by coloring your lines, letting them define a shape which may have its own, different color. (Skip Lawrence)

5. Use repetitive curvilinear lines for music-like statements or for action, and straight multidirectional lines for intense, active statements. (Marc Franz)

6. State distance with colored lines, close with warm colors, far with cool. (Leonardo da Vinci)

7. Use them to make patterns to pep up a large flat area. The stripe is a revered pattern and it's simply lines. (Henri Matisse)

8. Use a single outline to gather together a group of shapes which may otherwise not be unified - but once you do this you might need to continue the concept throughout the painting.

9. Introduce meandering lines to flat shapes to gain surface interest.

10. Finally, try to think of other ways to use line. It's great for the quick diagonal or curve in realistic work (electric lines in outdoor scenes or the edge of a background painting or ceiling/wall intersection in a figure or portrait), and its uses are only limited by your imagination. And aren't artists supposed to be imaginative?

Flat Out Art

What's the big deal with flattening in paintings? If you choose to take a workshop with me, George James, Skip Lawrence, Polly Hammett, or a dozen other folks, you'll have to flatten your people, houses, trees, lizards, whatever, because it's an assignment. But, I've noticed, even these sterling teachers (and I, too), sometimes forget to hammer home the reason for flattening. Here it is, in a nutshell:

It makes your composition easier to design/redesign.

Think about it. For realists, a composition as we see it is a complex set of objects (and the spaces between and/or around them) put together by hand or by visual selection to produce an aesthetic effect on a sheet of paper. And because of that complexity, we need to simplify it to really see the aesthetics. In other words, it's too damned hard to paint all that stuff and see if it makes a good design. So, what do we do?

If we flatten all the objects and show them as shapes, we can design the sheet as a group of shapes. That's nice, because you can assign value, color, texture and pattern to shapes and make them work together or apart as building blocks of design. It's really difficult to make a Persian flower pot and a group of different fruits work together because our tendency is to maintain the appeal of the objects, and not think of the big picture and the elements of design.

Here is a very simple and straightforward approach to composing a painting:

1. Clarify and simplify the shapes which make up the composition.

2. Add value to the shapes to begin to define where contrast is, what's in front of what, etc. - but still only as shapes.

3. Add color, but still maintain the value plan you've slaved over.

4. Vary and alter the shapes by size and outline to meet your own sensibilities about color and design. Which are biggest? How do they work with others? Can you remove some to simplify and improve the impact of the design? Do they balance? Is the design active, passive, reflective of your ideas about what you want to paint?

5. Ok, now that you've got the perfect composition, go back to the objects and see how you can clarify their identities by rounding, defining, but still maintaining the shapes you've just created.

Does this sound simple? Then wake up! This is the hard part about painting. It's the real art part, the reason Picasso stayed awake nights, and Rembrandt painted even when no one wanted to buy his work. Solving the design/feeling/appeal problem is what it's all about.

Watercolor (No Wimps, Please)

I just returned from my annual trek to Myrtle Beach, the preeminent watercolor workshop venue in the US. Nope, I didn't teach, but I attended a workshop by Carole Barnes, a wonderful abstract painter, primarily to learn acrylic techniques.

Now, some think if the painting doesn't show the hairs on the flies on the apple stem of the Red Delicious apple in the Ming china bowl on the 32 knot per inch Persian carpet, it must be abstract. *Au contraire*, the meaning of abstract and realism often bump into each other with surprising (and pleasing) results, and with the permissiveness in today's art world, there's no need to restrictively categorize work, other than for description's sake. I mean, at some level impressionism is an abstract form.

I find that many abstract painters *find* a composition while proceeding in their paintings, while others have a preconceived notion of the composition, but feel free to alter it while in the creative act. Meanwhile, some start from either end, but find a final concept somewhere in between. Some (Carole Barnes) use a theme to work through a painting, some (Carole again) use a series and apply titles during the painting to focus their intentions.

Mindset is important. I look for opportunities to change my paintings, realistic or abstract, as they proceed, as long as it makes them fresher and better. But I know my real strength is in color. So I study value, composition, line, shape, etc., before I commit paint to paper, then try to be intuitive in the color. That's where things develop that I never intended, and the place where I can let my senses take over.

You can do the same, but make an honest appraisal of your strengths, and look for opportunities there. Creating is not static, it's an act, and it takes courage. You may fail. Failures are stair steps to success, but only if you take the chance and learn from them. By considering each painting a work in progress, you lessen its preciousness. If you fail and need to start over, it's only another step on the way to success. And if you find an opportunity in the failure, you've not given up an inch in your journey.

So keep alert for opportunities - look for the boo-boos. Sometimes they can look really good if you try!

Composition from Another Point of View

"A basic structural design underlies every kind of painting. The painter will in part follow this design, in part deviate from it, according to the painter's skill, needs, and the unexpected needs that accompany the act of composition. Painting, to be effective, must follow closely the ideas of the painter, but not necessarily in the order in which those ideas occur. This calls for a scheme of procedure. In some cases the best design is no design... but in most cases planning must be a deliberate prelude to painting. The first principle of composition, therefore, is to foresee or determine the shape of what is to come, and pursue that shape."

The above piece on composition (with which I've taken some liberties) is concise, clearly stated, and true to the way we all work.

If you've suffered through my workshops or classes, you've heard my rant on how the arts all have elements common to their construction, notably, things like contrast and tension, which make for more interest and involvement by the viewer, audience, listener, etc. Composition, the one thing really common to all the arts, is the most difficult to teach, but easy to see once you've learned to look for it.

And all of the arts from music to literature to sculpture are really all about organizing shapes or sounds or ideas into something which is pleasant to the artist's eye, ear or psyche. That's composition - hard to teach because the minute you make a rule someone will break it and still have a <u>great</u> composition to show for it.

Well, why not? Isn't it all about balance? Isn't it all about "the shape of what is to come", and pursuing that shape? Can't get a handle on it? Well, however you go about it, when you get a composition you like and want to keep, figure out how it gets translated into a real painting. Don't slavishly copy the detail of your sketch, but follow the *scheme* for that composition, and let your artist's *informed intuition* determine the detail. That will retain the freshness and authority you seek as an artist.

Oh, and as to the authors of the above quote; simply substitute the word "writer(s)" or "writing" for "painter(s)" or "painting", and you'll have an exact quote from Strunk and White's *Elements of Style*, all about good writing. See what I mean when I say all the arts have common elements?

Bring Your Whips and Boots!

You never think of dominance in art, do you? Admit it! It's not a radical notion. You should know by now that virtually all art, from poetry to sculpture has common elements. One of those has to do with the *amounts* of whatever you paint (or write or compose musically or perform on stage) and how they compare to everything else in the piece.

The issue here is related to dominance (no, not the boots and whips kind), that is to say, what stands out most in your painting. Twenty or so years ago, I did a painting which was vaguely abstract, and which I thought had finally broken the barrier which stood between me and greatness. When I showed it to my accomplished friends, they responded that it was "interesting"...dangerous words for any artist, since they don't commit. I put the painting away for long while, and then took it out. The problem was, of course, all the shapes were the same size, all in complementary colors, and all fighting all over the painting. From across the room it was gray! No single shape or color was dominant. Moreover, there were no accents - and no interest whatsoever.

My lesson was clearly to start painting with different size shapes and organize color according to the role I wanted it to play in the painting. How? You can express dominance by size, shape, direction, color, value, texture, line, or pattern. Sound familiar? That's because (SURPRISE!) these are the elements of design.

There is no rule-book here, but I find it's easier for me to divide things into threes. Therefore, if I want value dominance, I think of three levels; dominant, subdominant and accent. The values can be dark, mid- or light tones. Color dominance can be expressed in hue, value, intensity or temperature. Use an intense red shape and other smaller shapes, more intense in color and your painting might get confused. I try to make the most dominant things take up the most space on the page, that way they are dominant because they're big. The subdominants take up the next bigger space, etc. until you put in accents, which are really a small, but significant part of the painting - they offer an alternative for the viewer's eye.

Invoke these ideas as you work, by evaluating (that's what the word "critique" means) works as you paint. Put them away for a while after you've finished, then look with fresh eyes, revise and - voilá! - anozer masterpiece weell be heading for ze museum!

How Much Should I Paint?

Someone wrote Katherine Anderson (answer-woman for *Watercolor Magic*) asking how much of the detail of a photograph he/she should paint? It's an engrossing question for those of us who work from photos. And I think it all depends on what you like. I can't possibly paint all the detail in a photo, mainly because I have a very short attention span, and get easily bored with detail. Some people thrive on it, and can produce a terrific painting with all the fly spots on the wall. They have my blessings.

Most of us are somewhere in between the swashing big-brush, get-it-all-down-in-twenty minutes painters and the flyspeck painters. So I try to find the art in the picture. If it's a photo, it's going to be chock full of stuff that may or may not add to the design and interest in a painting. Photography and painting are different mediums, and they speak in different ways to people. They are different languages and must be translated differently, with different inflections. Emphasis on certain parts in watercolor won't serve the same in photography.

I like to look for the design in the photo. I do this by trying to simplify and define the subject by shape and size. I put tracing paper over the photo and use a black pen to trace the shapes. I build a composition by adjusting what I see through the tracing paper. When I get that to my liking I overlay that base tracing with other overlays and begin carefully adding, subtracting, inventing, and re-inventing to come up with my own statement of what I liked about the original. From thereon I move to a sheet of watercolor paper and blow up the design I've worked through. I try to plan out the colors, values and "feel" of the piece I want to paint. Then I start and adjust as I move along. Sometimes I lose it - other times I move toward it until I find I'm finished.

Katherine's answer was that if you want a photograph when you finish your painting, why don't you just frame the original photo? Well, maybe some people like all that detail. I don't want to be so draconian, but if you want to move toward a more general approach to design, try mine. It's simple, but effective for me, (at least most of the time).

The Waterworks

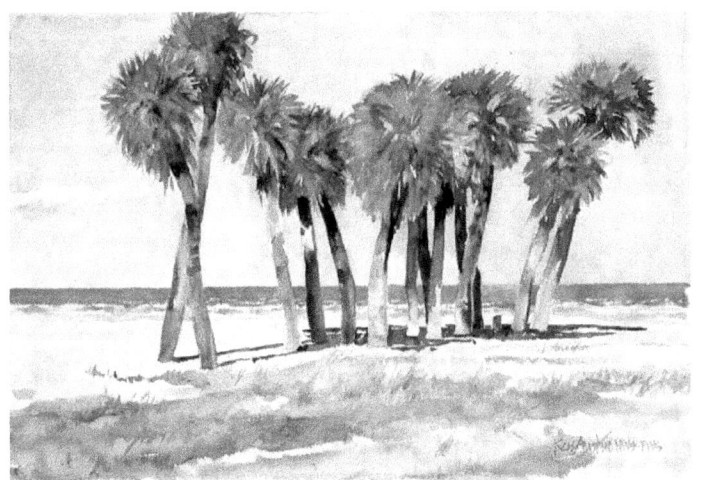

San Saba Dance

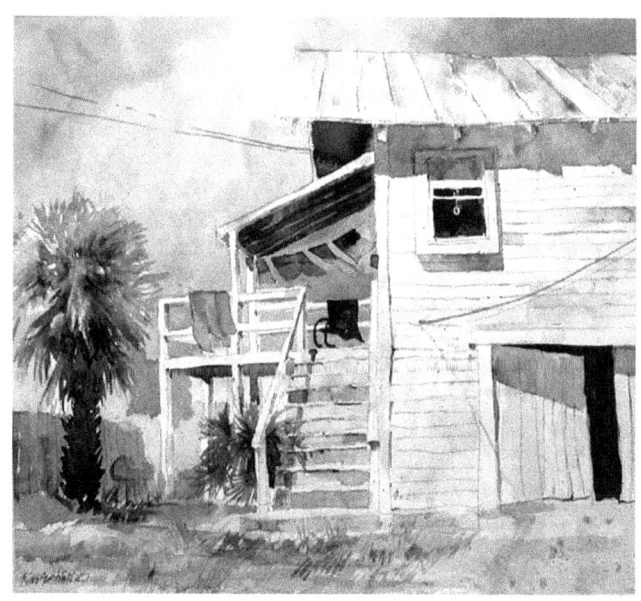

Key Ingredients

9
COMMUNITY CHEST

Familiar Feelings

There is a feeling like no other when you have accomplished something you've long wished for. Most of us get it early, when we've learned to read or learned to jump rope. That heady, "I can't believe it's real" feeling is the same one you get with your first inclusion in a local, state-wide, or national competition.

All that lightheaded, half relief, half joy, seasoned with wonderment feeling is a good thing, balky neurons notwithstanding, because it pushes us to feel we have to continue on that road, to do even better.

My first wins were in Houston with the Watercolor Art Society-Houston (WAS-H). I did an abstract at the annual Holidays Party and it won first place. Wow! After that I was juried into the annual membership show (a more austere and difficult effort because the membership was over 400, and many of them were superb artists with memberships in AWS and NWS). I still have that painting, a quarter sheet painting of a single white azalea blossom in a tiny vase. With continued study and support from my teachers, other artists and family, I managed to climb slowly in that sphere to the point where initials are less important than having what I paint recognized; which is a dicey issue at best. "Why?" you ask.

Because art, if not wholly in the eye of the beholder, is certainly one of the most personal and subjective things in the world. And, because of that subjectivity our self-images might suffer a ding now and then. So what makes art- uh- art?

A philosopher I'm not, but I have a theory that as artists we don't need to be involved in the ultimate definition of art. It's better if we make art and let others talk about it. If one man's art is another man's junk, is the opposite true? (See the Duchamp urinal from 1917.)

But over the years I've thought about what we *call* art, and here's my little input into the whole messy, weird discussion: What we call art depends on what our involvement is in the art world. For me there are three groups that influence what is called art. The first is the *artists* themselves, surely the most liberal thinkers when it comes to calling something art. Because pretty much anything anybody *calls* art is, to artists, art. We don't down-talk anyone's art for fear that someone will down-talk ours…except in private with friends who think the same as we do.

Second in line is what *critics* call art. Many critics aren't artists at all, but they judge and value art in news articles, books and online, exercising a sway on the art-loving public (yes, there is one out there!), and affecting the popularity and monetary value of an artist's work by what they have to say about it – specifically, if it's art or not.

Finally, the largest group is the *public*. The public in America is not the public in Europe when it comes to art. Our public grew up in the 1800s with little access to art museums, art exhibits or galleries. The result was that art was what they saw as illustrations and advertisements in newspapers, magazines, rich people's homes and public facilities. As a result our general public has had a guarded acceptance of abstract, pop, surreal, or any art category other than representational works until recently, when urban populations outgrew rural ones, and there was better education and more opportunity to see, learn about, and become accustomed to contemporary art.

"So what?" you say. Well, it is important to remember that when you enter a show, you can't guess what the judges will like, or what the audience will like, but you can be pretty sure that other artists, while having opinions on your work, will never put your work or you down (to your face anyhow) for what you've tried to create.

There is an informative road to take, however; try to find what the judge liked or felt could be *improved* in your work, what other artists with opinions you value recommend as improvements, as well as what the public sees in it. The first two are easy to find; just ask. The public is harder to deal with because the quality of their responses is broad and personal, and they might not be around for you to question. But if you can get a sense of how your work will be received by all three groups, and if you can find in their responses ways to *improve* your art, you might get a better handle on how to make your art more accessible and better.

Remember, even though the history of art is a history of rebellion and change, time leaves us with works made great by eventually softening everyone's objections to them through familiarization. That great, talkative watercolor art teacher, Ed Whitney, collected witticisms in a small notebook he kept with him at all times.

One night in Houston, over a glass of wine, discussing *learning* about all kinds of art, I told him that my belief was that, "familiarity breeds content". He leaned forward, took out his pen, smiled, and said, "That's going in my collection".

Stepping In

This is a special piece by my wonderful daughter, Elizabeth King Gerlach. "Lizzie" is a gifted author and photographer. Among other articles and essays, was this short piece for one of the "Hero Series," from Adams Media, "My Dad Is My Hero". It's a lovely, touching picture of how a small act can help someone when they need it. I think you'll all enjoy it - especially the dads!

While many macho East Texas dads turned red-in-the-face from screaming for their favorite football team and eating too much *chili con quéso*, my stepdad could be found quietly exploring the many angles of how light hits a bluebonnet.

Every weekend in his make-shift studio, a hallway room, he diligently washed delicate colors over white paper and pencil sketches. He was teaching himself how to watercolor. Reams of discarded paper cluttered his desk and the floor. "Studies" were tacked up on the wall and hung to dry on an indoor clothesline. How many ways can you paint a primrose? On any given Sunday at our house, about 557 and counting...

Ken worked a day job with the city, and pulled in what it takes to "put bread on the table." But his true interest lay in painting that bread and perhaps a glass of wine, in a still life. He also loved music and taught us chords on the guitar. Many nights we would get together and listen to him pick bluegrass classics or strum folk songs. We learned how to sing along, even if we never quite became the next Von Trapp Family singers.

It is only in retrospect that I understand how much he undertook when he married my mom. She was a "single-mom" when those two words weren't a familiar pairing, way back in the late 1960s. She had escaped an emotionally abusive husband, with three fragile little kids in tow, and was desperately trying to make a new life for herself and for us.

He must have been crazy in love with her. (I'm pretty sure he still is.) They met in graduate school and were married outside near a lake, with flowers in their hair. We kids baked them a Betty Crocker wedding cake with "Mom + Ken = Love 4 Ever" piped on the top. I'm sure we fought about who got to frost it.

My siblings and I fought constantly, vied for attention every minute of the day and took out our competitive urges over long games of Monopoly. Someone inevitably stormed off at the end of the game, vowing to never play again. Nothing about our family life was either idyllic or perfect.

Somehow he managed to weather all the drama. Focusing on his art and music probably kept him sane. We learned to give him lots of time and space for this, sometimes resenting the fact that he spent so much time on it, but nevertheless we understood it was important.

Ken loved art, and he also loved to share his love of art. He encouraged all of us to explore our creative sides. He insisted we visit churches and museums and from him we learned terms like "vernacular" and "fresco" not to mention the meaning of inspiration. He filled our house with art books. Who was this Monet, and why couldn't he draw a straight line?

My stepdad helped me get my first job at a small newspaper when I was only fifteen. It was there that my love of photography and writing began to blossom. Ken helped me set up my own dark room, took me to photo shows and explained the basics of composition and contrast.

Near the end of my senior year, I set my sights on entering a national photo competition. Still, as the deadline for the contest came down to the wire, I could not complete the necessary steps to enter. Perhaps due to deep feelings of inadequacy and unworthiness, the day before the contest came around and I had still had not mailed the photographs.

That was when my stepdad stepped in. Maybe he had been holding back, waiting and watching for me to take responsibility. But at the eleventh hour, he said to me, "This is a big deal and your work is good. I'm not going to let you blow it. There is such a thing as overnight mail!"

And he mailed them off for me.

It was a small act of love, but a great act of faith. My photos won several categories and ultimately I was given a college scholarship. To this day, I don't think that I would have the confidence to be a writer if it wasn't for my stepdad stepping in. His belief in me, even when I couldn't believe in myself, opened doors for me and gave me confidence to carry on.

It's not only his belief in me that makes him my hero, but also the way he believes in the importance of following your heart. Over the years, his consistency and commitment to his art and his music has won him many friends and awards. But even beyond that it's his quiet persistence in following his own passion that has given others permission to follow theirs.

A good painting, like life, has a nice balance of elements. Sometimes the flower is in the foreground, popping with color and stealing the show. Sometimes the flowers are in the field, acting as a supporting cast. Yes, my stepdad taught me that there are a thousand ways to see a flower, and when I needed him the most, he stepped in and showed me that *I was the flower.*

"Stepping In" by Elizabeth King Gerlach reprinted from *My Dad is My Hero* edited by Susan Reynolds, Copyright © 2009 by Susan Reynolds. Used by permission of Adams Media, an F+W Media, Inc. Company. All rights reserved.

The Tempest

A storm is brewing. I do not mean the Shakespearean tragedy kind, but one that could be disappointing for some, depending on how it's resolved. As happened sixteen years ago, there is a rebellion among some Florida Watercolor Society members against allowing non-pure watercolor paintings in FWS annual shows. Specifically, it's because there was a record proportion of acrylic paintings winning awards in the most recent show, and generally because some members want the name of "watercolor" to become "transparent watercolor".

I wrote a tome for *the American Artist Magazine's* artists' forum, which you may read at your leisure. The issue is being discussed there now, and you may join the discussion.

My point of view (call me liberal) is that "watercolor" has always been inclusive of gouache, egg tempera, colored inks, etc....all the way from Sargent, Homer, Kandinsky, to Wyeth, Hopper, and others. They would all be welcomed into FWS shows now, but not with a delimiting description of allowable pigment. To further limit now will have several ill effects on the Society as well as many members.

Here's why I believe this:
-It will eventually strangle the innovative spirit of many members who are some of the best artists in the group, and in the nation, and thus are a credit to the FWS.

-Show awards aren't made on the basis of medium, but on quality of painting.

-American Watercolor Society and the National Watercolor Society, the preeminent show groups in the nation allow acrylic, gouache, etc.

-I know pure watercolor can win top prizes because Steve Rogers, who is a consummate artist in pure watercolor, wins top awards in the nation's best shows that allow "impure" paintings. (In fairness, he disagrees with my point of view, however.)

In my response I also posit that I see two answers to the issue:

-Demand a specific percentage of pures be selected in each show (you might not get a juror who agrees to that, and you'll have a never-ending fight over the correct percentage) or,

-Paint better paintings in transparent watercolor (a radical notion, I know, but we're being open here!)

I'm writing this because I know our CFWS has wrestled with the same issues and will again. Our bylaws (which I drafted, for better or worse) are shamelessly based on FWS's bylaws, so the definition of "watercolor" is the same, and this sort of issue will be raised again (as it already has).

In a month or so there will be a poll of FWS members on these issues. I have not written this to goad any CFWS folks who are members of FWS into my point of view, but in order to ask that all give thoughtful consideration to all aspects of this situation. Both sides are valid in some degree, so try to work through where you stand as an artist and as a member of FWS, *and* of CFWS.

And then vote your conscience. Vote the same as I will. (Okay, just kidding!!)

The Tempest II

My watercolor society recently came to grips with the problem of the century! Now you can enter the annual show with watercolor on paper, board, clayboard, canvas, Yupo – virtually anything that says it's made for watercolor. While my tone is sarcastic, the issue is important to a host of people who love the annual competition, but feel their best work is on Yupo or clayboard instead of Arches 140#. They felt excluded. Formerly only works on paper were accepted until Yupo reared its ugly head. FWS had to allow Yupo because some prominent watercolorists a few years back painted on Yupo exclusively. But then, in quick succession came issues about entering work on watercolor canvas, clayboard, mounted paper, etc., etc. What to do?

This was an issue only because some members wanted to accept paintings on other supports than paper. Of course, some members would like to see only transparent watercolor used; no gouache, no acrylic, etc. On the other hand, there may be some who'd like to see water-based oils allowed as well, and some who'd like to not use glass on submissions. The list goes on and on.

I try to stay out of such dustups, because I don't care. I paint in several media, mixing and matching as I go, but always on paper (at least to date). I don't much care what others use as a ground, as long as it has something to do with water in paint.

Maybe that is not a really good benchmark, but I did not invent watercolor competitions. I don't know who did, but the American Watercolor Society was started in 1866 "to promote the art of watercolor painting in America." In 1866 people were painting in "watercolor with body color", a nice term for transparent color mixed with Chinese White to make it opaque. Thomas Eakins, Winslow Homer, John Singer Sargent, all painted this way, as J. M. W. Turner had 50 years prior.

Sometimes they gave up and painted in gouache, sometimes in all-transparent watercolor. Transparency wasn't precious. Nobody cared. Nobody kept them from exhibiting, but then *their* competition was not a contest to see who's best, but who could sell. And watercolor on paper was not as marketable as oils on canvas (well, except maybe for Homer's work).

So what, you say? It's about competition, says I!

My students know of my low regard for rules in art. So when competition rules don't suit you, don't enter. Griping is fine, however. I love the way our group resolved the support issue by taking a vote from members - democracy at work! And another vote will arise someday, when tastes, materials, attitudes and methods of painting change enough.

Believe it or not, change is inevitable in everything, watercolor included. And it tells me there's room for *everybody's* work in watercolor, regardless of how you paint and what the support is.

So I suggest you sit back, relax, and go on toward your personal goals in painting. If you decide oils are the real deal, go for it. If you like painting like John Pike or Ted Kautzky in watercolor, do it! It's only paint on paper. You have a right to do with it what you like. Enjoy it!

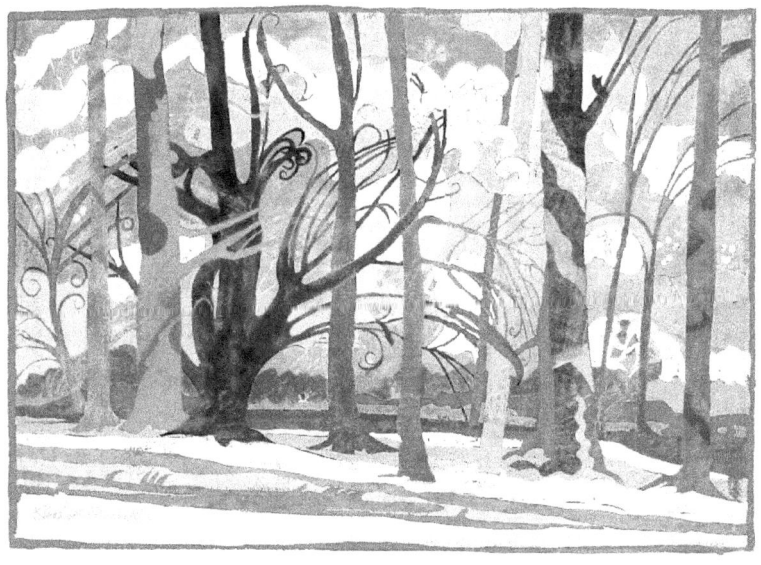

A Walk In the Woods

Complimentary Colorings

A few years ago I was in a workshop with the great Skip Lawrence, and had made acquaintances with a woman who sat across the aisle from me.

We both struggled through Skip's assignments together, and she seemed very nice and very dedicated to watercolor, though a less experienced artist than I.

Skip had asked us to bring slides for a critique, and had been through them with us one-on-one, then began showing them to the group as a whole. When he came to my paintings, they generated considerable discussion in the class (which was ok with me), since they are anything but standard figures, designs and techniques.

As we left the projection room, my newfound friend said to me, "Gosh, Ken, I liked your work so much!" I thanked her and told her how much I appreciated her compliments.

"You know," she said, "I never suspected you painted like that - I mean - I just thought you were a normal person!"

I still appreciate what she said and how she said it.

Moral: Sometimes what people don't mean to say is more important than what they think they are saying.

Soul Food Recipe

Recently, because of the energy, interest and initiative of my friend and sometimes student, Chere, she and three others of us took a road trip to Bradenton's ArtCenter Manatee to see the National Watercolor Society (NWS) traveling show. This show is from the NWS, one of the most prestigious watercolor societies in the U.S. To be a signature member your painting must be juried into their annual show and then more of your work assessed to be sure you're qualified. The show we saw was composed of a part of the NWS annual open show, basically those paintings which the artists allowed to be in the traveling show.

The quality and beauty of these works always makes them a lesson in watercolor art. The "wow" factor was definitely there for us, as well as some other lessons we didn't expect. First, there was the variety of supports and surfaces painted on, including: Yupo, bristol board, hot, cold and rough watercolor papers, and paper prepared with gesso. Next, the variety of paints used, including transparent watercolor, acrylic, gouache, and possibly casein (we couldn't really tell), along with bits of collage, colored pencil, pastel, and ink. Also, techniques ranged from pure traditional watercolor on paper to a painting in transparent acrylic over collage. Finally, as in all competitions, the range of subject matter was from real to abstract to surreal to visionary to as yet unnamed. We didn't all like all of them. But we agreed even those we didn't like were well done. Concepts, styles, and subjects don't always work for us as individuals. But here the quality was admirable and educational.

So, what was the common thread that made all these paintings so special that they won out over 1200 others for a place in the sun? Here are my ideas: first, all of the artists were in complete technical control of their work. They knew what they were doing and how best to achieve results in a way that supported the themes and ideas that made their paintings stand out. They also knew how to present their paintings. Frames and mats varied, but the painting was always the main thing to see, and it always showed itself admirably. Finally, they had great *originality* in the selection and presentation of their subjects. You know this when you keep thinking, "I *never* would have thought of *that*!"

Our outing was a great success (even with my bad recommendation for a lunch place!) More importantly, I think the trip was good for feeding our artists' souls. Seeing the best work in the nation, the state, or central Florida will always be an enlightening, educational, and exciting experience. And discussing it will be even more so. I hope you will take yourself and some friends on your own "soul food" adventure sometime!

Lasting Influences

We never know whom we influence or exactly how. In fact, the opposite is sometimes the case as well; often we don't really know who has influenced us. Now, when I say this, I don't mean that we don't know those big influences – family, teachers, best friends, etc. – all the obvious ones. But sometimes those influences are subtle, but lasting, and this serves in art as well as other areas of our lives.

What brought this to mind was the recent loss of one of this area's great figures in the art world; Louise Peterson. Louise, along with Judy Albertson (another unsung art hero) owned and operated the Albertson – Peterson Gallery in the old Colony Theatre on Park Avenue in Winter Park, FL.

This was the first gallery I was invited to exhibit in, and when I got the invitation I was near ecstasy because I had previously visited the gallery many times (once to see a show of Steven Rogers' work), and thought it showed the best mix of styles and talents I had seen in Florida. Not only that, but Louise and Judy were absolutely convinced that my work would be perfect for the gallery, a great compliment to me. Nonetheless, while my work (those crazy big nude females) didn't exactly fly off the walls, the gallery's enthusiasm didn't languish, and so we continued our relationship over about 10 or 12 years, until their closing. At one of our occasional lunches I asked why she thought my work sold so slowly. In her gravelly, metered voice, she said simply, "Well, Ken, I just don't think people in this area want big nude women looking down from the walls of their dining rooms." 'Nuff said.

I would see Louise in the years following their closing, usually in chance meetings at art events, in stores, etc. She was, as always, genuinely interested in my progress in art, thrilled at any positive report, and full of information and advice if I wanted any. She was also generous in lecturing at Comma Gallery, and made herself available for other art-related functions. But our meetings became less frequent as my life became more involved in my day-job, painting and family matters.

I now regret not taking time to keep up with her, and, as is often the case, I'm mulling over how someone I've worked with, but is now gone, has impacted my life. I'm still painting those big women. Maybe they don't sell so well, but they win awards in national competitions, and I might have given up on them if Louise hadn't had such faith in me. I know her faith wasn't because of the money. But I also know that for most of those 10 years of showing my work, she kept one of my paintings hanging over the desk in her office – because, as she professed, she loved it.

Not many artists can say that, and looking back I now know it helped keep me going for quite a while when I most needed it.

That's influence.

Art Is Serious (Or Not?)

Are you ready for more bracing art discussion, learning and painting? And anyone who says "Nah" is not serious about art. But actually, I have a few issues about seriousness in art.

Last month I was at the Florida Watercolor Society's 34th Annual Exhibition opening and convention. At the awards banquet I sat next to accomplished artists whose work I knew from previous shows. And, making the rounds, I saw professionals (Steve and Janet Rogers, Jean Grastorf, Jeanne Dobie, and the Juror, George James) whose work has been in plenty of shows all over the U.S. (and, wow! - can they paint!).

People are often judged as serious or not serious artists. The "serious" term is pretty broad, meaning everything from producing giant paintings to starving while you get good enough to have a full-time career in art. Meanwhile, millions of others are happily painting everything from puppies to pachyderms and, for them, serious art is how you get *just the right* tin roof color. That's a big gulf, and it seems an overly important one to me.

I have a friend who's the director of a prestigious art museum, and one day not long ago we went to lunch together. He was not in a great mood and when I got him to unload to me, he confided he'd had a committee meeting all morning and that 90% of it revolved around one member and that member's objections to one piece of art. Finally, in exasperation, my friend the director said to him, "Oh, for God's sake, John, IT'S ONLY ART!"

Now, that's what I call a healthy attitude. No bloviating, no sanctification, no critical judgment, just an observation on one single aspect - it's art, no more, no less.

We all need to think about whether what we do is art. It's basic. And somehow, I think we need to realize that if it's not art now, that's no sin; we can do another painting and it may well be art. The tendency to glorify all things to do with art is often just another way to *exclude* people. I prefer to see people *included*. I hope you do too.

On Workshops

We CFWS members have a lot to be thankful for. We have access to monthly social/educational gatherings, opportunities to meet others in our field, sharing our interests with different people at different levels, and an opportunity to learn first-hand from experienced well-known artists from this area as well as other parts of the nation.

Of all these opportunities, the last is probably the most important, at least in terms of meeting our major goal and purpose as an organization. And it's the reason the organization was formed in the first place. It was a slam-dunk that if we started it, they would come.

I haven't counted, over the years, how many workshops we've had, but I have yet to hear that anyone griped about low quality of information or lesson value. I think that part is working pretty well. I know because I hear first-hand from my classes and my workshop participants. But what I also see and hear is that there's some reduction in the numbers taking workshops. Maybe it's the economy, or maybe it's some other ill-scheduled events vying for your attention, but we, as an organization need to be fully aware that workshops don't come for free.

For those of you who don't know, a workshop is sometimes based on the number of students attending, sometimes on a flat rate per day, sometimes on a combination of factors. Any way you cut it, teachers get paid for teaching plus expenses. In general, the more famous the teacher, the more it costs the CFWS to get them here. There's a set contract time for cancellation, so we need as many early up-front commitments from students as we can get. So, more students early on means more money guaranteed for the instructor and less stress for those running the workshop.

And speaking of workshop managers, we need volunteers for assistance with workshops (and other offices on the Board). These jobs aren't easy, but some perks are included; you get to know the instructor pretty well, and you can take the workshop for free. Not a bad deal, I'd say.

Finally, let me tell you that I have profited more from workshops myself than any other form of art education except for sharing a studio with a major artist. The workshop atmosphere is one of discovery, practice, learning, and seeing major talent at work when demos or lectures fire you to explore and improve. You learn from what others do, from what you fail or succeed in doing, and from the experience itself.

Remembrances

A call from the Watercolor Art Society – Houston (WAS-H) a few weeks back brought some pride and happiness. I lived 12 years in Houston, TX, six of which were spent serving on the Board of Directors of this fine organization, eventually as president. And now, after 25 years they are proposing to their board to have me teach a workshop, and demonstrate for their meeting. Nice praise for the guy who started out setting up the demo mirror for two years.

For those of you who don't know, being president of a watercolor society is a tough task, usually one that narrows down to whoever will agree to serve. It is a full-time job, one that needs support from the entire organization, especially from others who will give their time and efforts to serve as board members. Board members in major corporations are paid in money, stock and comps for their services. Ours are paid in good wishes and thanks for jobs well done.

I turned down the request to be CFWS president, because I didn't want this group to be a copy of its Houston counterpart. The Orlando area has its own sensibility and direction, so people of this area should be the ones directing our society's growth and development. Our annual holiday meeting proved how well we've met that vision. The inclusive camaraderie and personal involvement of the board and membership was a joyful expression of this organization's mutual love for all things watercolor.

In Houston, I can remember seeing work by advanced painters in the WAS-H membership and open shows, wondering if I'd ever be in one, and the joy I felt when my work was finally accepted. It would be several years before I'd qualify for an open show, but the fire was fed by the combination of that early entry into the world of the "big kids" and their compliments on my paintings.

I have students whose primary interest is to compete, and it drives their desire to learn and perfect their work in watercolor. Others want to learn to express their vision of what their art should, could, or would be if they only had the skill to produce it. Some just want to enjoy the activities and the social involvement of the group they paint with. Some want to paint like specific artists (though they seldom admit it and seldom maintain that dream).

I've always loved the feeling I have when a painting's headed in the right direction. Knowing I'm producing something I conceived, initiated, and know how to make whole is an exciting and worthwhile effort for me. That's why the CFWS is so rewarding to watch, developing and succeeding on so many levels. And like any good artist knows, there's a time to step back and put your brush down.

I'm happy I stepped back early on. The void has been filled admirably, with the dedicated work of people just like you – yes, just like you, not schooled in organizational how-to, but with dedication to the goals of our society.

I hope those of you who enjoy your own local watercolor society will consider stepping forward to fill vacancies in the future. You'll not only help keep these important groups active and growing, but you'll help yourself and your painting friends to learn, enjoy and excel at what they love. And I guarantee, the memories are worth it all.

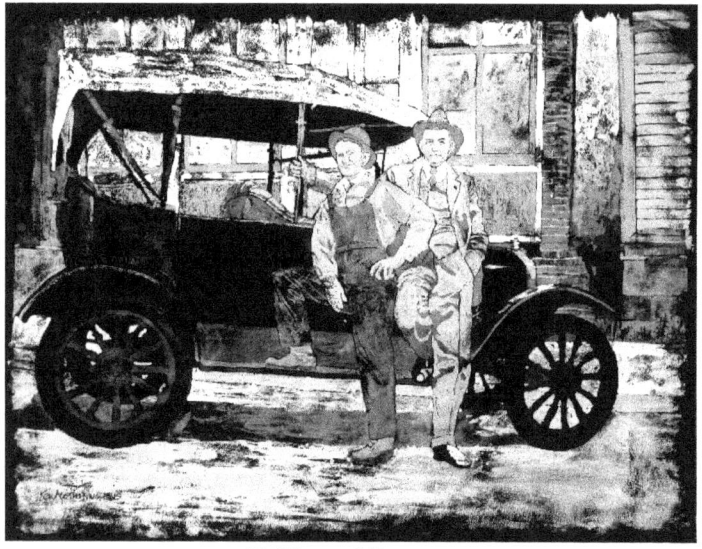

Willy and Bascom

10
KEEP AN OPEN MIND

Art Is Backward

Did you know Peter Falk (remember "Colombo"?) had an art education and was a very fine artist in addition to being a wonderful actor? He drew women, and what wonderful drawings they are! Well, I read a story he told wherein:

An artist, whose studio was atop his garage, was painting a nude study with a live female model. Things weren't going well, so he suggested they take a break. She put on her robe, and they sat down to cup of coffee at the table overlooking the driveway. After chatting a few minutes he saw a car turn into the drive, jumped up and said, "Quick, it's my wife - take your clothes off, or she might think we're up to something!"

This led me to some deep thought- ok, not so deep- concluding that art is backward like that. Think of it:

-Most people see art they love, and buy it. Artists make art they love, and sell it.

-Most people paint walls colors they love, and then find paintings to match. Artists make paintings they love then paint the walls to match.

-Most people view the world as something to be dealt with. Artists view the world as something to create with.

-Most people view art as something they can't do. Artists view art as something they must do.

-Most people think of art as something they can live without. Artists think of art as something they can't live without.

-Most people buy art and hang it on the wall. Artists hang art on the wall and sell it.

-Most people struggle to describe the color of things. Artists struggle to describe things by using color.

Now all this doesn't mean everybody fits one mold or the other. Many of us are really as good at the left as the right brain. But I get the sense that, in spite of the world's seemingly negative view of the artist as head-in-the-clouds, impractical, societal hanger-ons, the fact is we're just different. And don't forget, someone actually paid money for Michelangelo to paint the Sistine Chapel!

So go forward, you leagues of artists, with your tongues firmly planted in your cheeks, and remember, the rest of the world pays for the abuse heaped upon us by buying the beauty we put into their lives.

Finding Your Way

The subject of this essay is: YOU!

I've had dozens of students/artists in my classes and workshops, others getting critiques, and quite a few others who just ask me, "What do you think of this painting?". It's not always easy to evaluate a painting in a short time, and to give someone a positive answer isn't always easy. It's not like seeing someone and saying, "My, you look nice today!" The art people make is *part of them*. It's not a separate thing, like a paint-by-the-numbers piece, so one must be truthful and honest in an assessment without being negative or overbearing or personal. (I realize not all teachers share my opinion, but that's their way of teaching, not mine).

Because of this I often see students who have done a pretty good job, but are not able to recognize their achievements. It's easy to feel defeated and deflated when you've worked hard to achieve something that's not as great as you thought it was. We live in a culture that thrives on instant gratification, but making good art doesn't come that fast. It takes time, practice, technique, knowledge, and lots of experience. So being patient isn't a virtue – it's a necessity!

Still, I find students often don't realize that the learning process is incremental in art. And if we're lucky, it continues that way throughout our time here. So, in the interest of all you learning artists out there, I've created a short list of questions/statements for you.

They aren't an exam; they're for you to gauge your depth of interest, knowledge and commitment to your art. There are no "right" or "wrong" answers, except in your own expectations of yourself. I hope these will give you some insight into your own likes, dislikes, prejudices, goals, etc. When you've had time to think about these things you'll likely want to move in a different direction in some areas and strengthen your skills in others. Try writing down your answers and leaving them for a day or two before you look at them again. Then you'll be better equipped to make some notes or put together a plan for how to improve your art.

Remember, it's not just, "does it *look* like it?" It's always, "does it *feel* like it?"

- Who's really your intended audience?
    Your friends/family?
    Your fellow artists?
    Critics/Judges?
    The public?
    Yourself only?
    All of the above?

- Do you tell yourself out loud what you like about your paintings?

- Do you like to try out new ideas/styles/kinds of paintings?

- If you could change one thing about your work, what would it be?

- Do you like detail and specificity in your painting?

- Do you like "loose handling" in watercolor?

- Are you familiar with great watercolor painters' styles and lives?

- Are you familiar with other great artists' styles and lives?

- Do you try to emulate them? In what ways?

- Do you try out suggestions from books on painting?

- Do you go to workshops?

- Do you sketch a lot? Photograph a lot for paintings?

- Do you enter competitions?

- Do you want recognition, money, both, or neither, for your work - or do you just love doing it? (You can have all three if you're lucky!)

How do you learn best?

 -Live teacher(s), Videos

 -Books

 -By watching others paint?

Are you a "realist", or an "abstractionist"? Are you a "color painter" or a "value painter"? Do you paint big or little? Do you understand Matisse's statement; "When I put a green, it is not grass. When I put a blue, it is not the sky."

Think about it!

How Much Are YOU Worth?

I'm sure I'll be labeled a pariah for this, but I think it's worth airing. The other day I received an email asking me to donate a painting to a charitable organization's auction/fundraiser.

Now, I try to be charitable and supportive of all kinds of community fundraisers, and I donate money to favorites every year, some by way of paid membership, some with extra cash. I believe strongly in volunteer efforts and generosity in charity efforts such as this - at least in most of them. But I must admit, I have a hard spot when it comes to donating art. Here's why.

If my paintings were worth $50,000 each, and my annual income from painting was a couple of million a year, I'd gladly donate a painting, or, maybe a drawing, or print, etc. But the fact is, my annual income from painting won't put a new room on my house. And my income from workshops is only slightly better.

Ninety-five percent of the artists I know are in the same boat or worse. They struggle to pay for rent, materials, receptions at shows, framing, you name it. But they are all asked to donate their art for charity. They almost all donate and I think they should do what they believe is fair. But the people who bid on and buy these works almost always get a bargain.

The donating artist is led to think this is great advertisement, or a marketing opportunity, but I've never had a sale due to my work being seen or sold in a charity auction. Am I sounding selfish? Maybe.

On the other hand, I've never seen a dentist asked to donate a new crown for auction, or a surgeon to offer a heart bypass, or a free emergency call from a plumbing company, or a free will from an attorney. Why not? Aren't there usually surgeons and lawyers on boards of charitable organizations? Wouldn't those be expensive things people really want? Wouldn't you bid a couple of hundred for cataract surgery? So why do we artists offer up our goods like sheep? Because we are suckers, that's why.

We want to help so badly that we play along. We give away hours of our valuable time and years of experience in the form of our art for nothing. The last time I donated art the value of the frame was $120, I valued the painting and frame at $350 and it sold at $60. This does not flatter me or make me feel like I've done something smart or of great benefit. I would much rather donate $60.

Since that time I either don't respond or, more often I suggest that if the organization wants artists to donate they should get other *professionals* to donate services/products as well *or*, better, let donating artists set a starting bid which would pay them a fair minimum they would want from the work, even if it's below market.

This week I was asked for a painting by an organization that helps children with autism. My oldest grandson has autism, and it has been a life-affirming experience to know him and the kind of work and courage he has shown in order to take his place as an individual of value in the world. It was hard, but I didn't give them a painting. I will donate cash – and this article as a letter of explanation.

Seven Deadly Sins

No, I'm not preaching (well, maybe just a little), but I find that as I reach middle age (okay, just kidding) there are some constants keeping some of us from advancing in our pursuit of painting. They are:

1. Procrastination

2. Self-Degradation

3. No Place of My Own

4. Do It Yourself

5. Holding Back

6. Detail Derailment

7. Self-Deception

Here we go:

1. *Procrastination* is the bane of all who need to progress. Why? You can't progress standing still. How to combat it? Experts will give you a longer and better list than I. Therapists will work it out for you for $$$/hr. Babies teach you a lesson quickly. But here's my theory. Find what you love about painting. Build on it. Make it a *really BIG* part of your life. Enjoy what you create, and enjoy creating it even more. Then

you'll not want to wait for an opportunity to arise, you'll make the opportunity by putting it on your calendar just like you would the other things you do. Do you use a calendar? If not, you'll want to make it a habit.

2. *Self-degradation* comes from our parents (or others) telling us to be modest. So we all deny our good works and classify all our painting efforts as "really not very good', or "just awful", or "I don't really know what I'm doing." We will say anything to deny our abilities at art. We shouldn't say we are artists unless we are little Michelangelos.

The fact is that most of us were artistically stunted when we were about 12 or 13. We had a natural response to others' talents because we were finding out that they could do things (art) way better than we could, and we didn't want to be embarrassed about *anything* so we looked for things we *could* do at least as well as our group. Which means (unless your group was a school for the arts) that you'd rather have sat on the sidelines being afraid than painting something not as good as someone else could paint. Well, GET OVER IT. Just start. Just finish. If you come to my class, I assume you don't know how to do this stuff. If you did, why would you be in my class? So, please, give yourself the benefit of a doubt. You'll learn in small doses, just like we all did. But you can't learn if you always belittle yourself and your work as "no good".

3. *No place of your own* (to paint in), means you have a great excuse not to paint – "It's just too much trouble to get all my stuff out and put it away when I'm done." And that means you can't paint. Because you never get your stuff out to paint. No paint no practice. Like the man playing sax for coins on the corner in New York, when asked by a tourist, "How do I get to Carnegie Hall?" He said, "Practice, young man, practice!" You can't practice without your stuff! Get a card table and leave your stuff out. You'll find you can't resist the siren call of Cerulean Blue or Permanent Rose!

4. *Do-it-yourself* fans just won't believe that anyone could help them do something better, or that it might cost some money, or maybe they believe that art is all about feeling and doing, not about learning. Maybe you're different from me, but I learned how to make my paintings better when I started taking lessons. Why? The secret is: there is no secret! If you never once went to school would you be able to read, write, add, subtract, or do nuclear physics (ok, maybe not the last one)? Just because you raised three stepchildren and built a new barn while holding down a business you created doesn't mean you can't benefit from a little education. It's there. Take the leap and stop being too proud/stubborn to bare your ignorance. If you're a great painter, why aren't you producing great paintings?

5. *Holding Back* is a problem for many of us. We don't want to let ourselves go because we might be

embarrassed at what we expose. Or, we might do the wrong thing. Or we just can't believe we could really do anything good! Well, get over it! You'll find if you get serious about the art you'll not be judged by what other artists think of *you*, but what they think *of the art* you produce! Now, wouldn't it be great to be a real crank, but be loved because of your art? (Good luck on that – but the idea is still valid.)

6. *Detail Derailment* is a common occurrence among artists who want to be better but can't. We get so wrapped up in painting every strawberry in the still life, every hair on the dog, every letter on the newspaper in the background, that we (literally) lose the picture. But let me give you a well-learned warning – no one can look at a painting with every square inch of it full of infinite detail and stand it for more than 10 seconds. Our eyes (brains, that is) don't see detail unless they want to. When that happens detail is still contained in a small percentage of all we see.

Don't believe it? Just tell me what you can see in the four corners of your computer screen or this book when you look at the period ending this sentence. Ha! I stand on my observation. So, provide detail information only when you want the viewer to have the details. You don't have to show every hair on every gnat on every ear on every person signing the Declaration of Independence. Think about it and forget it. You'll find the pathway to successful paintings depends on painting only the information the viewer needs to understand what your painting is about.

Work from the specific to the general in concept sketches (I want to paint a boat scene). Work from the general to the specific on the final painting (this boat needs less rigging than I see in the photo).

7. *Self-Deception* is the road to hell in watercolor. Thinking that what you're doing is wrong because it was wrong when you were in kindergarten is NOT a good reason to shy away from it as an adult. Think of all the other things that were wrong before you were an adult. Lots of them turned out not wrong at all, and some ended up being way too much fun! It's the same with art.

It is okay to color outside the lines. (Believe me, it's true, Cinderella). On the other hand, believing that something is right just because you're breaking the rules won't work either. Being the rule breaker won't make you a good artist any more than driving at 120 mph will make you a good race car driver. So don't deceive yourself about who you are or what you *must do* in the maelstrom of art. Just try to do the best painting you can.

In short, the most important thing is the search for *your personal* statement. The how and what of it are the stuff of art. It doesn't have to be new, great, insightful, magnificent, contemporary, or perfect. It just has to let others know how you feel or view or think about something through the historic filter of visual design. And that, as they say, ain't easy. But you can get there.

The Lost Painting

My flat file is an ancient oak affair with drawers that don't work and a top that sags. It's full of old paintings, booklets, other attendant memorabilia, minutiae and a lot of stuff I've forgotten about. In a recent search for a work to illustrate value-based painting for my class, I also found a painting I did in 1989 which was surprisingly good. Now this is "good" by my own standard, and, while it may have flaws, it has much to be enjoyed if not admired. It's a simple still life, a study of some office stuff on a table with some crumpled paper as part of the scene. It's realistic, and colorful, and reasonably appealing, but mostly I remember painting this full sheet in only two and half hours. It occurred how we sometimes give up good things to get where we'd rather be.

Since 1989 my painting has morphed into more precise, labor intensive work, where I agonize over each brushstroke, and constantly evaluate how the whole thing holds together. And while better in a sense, the newer paintings don't have that spontaneity that the older painting has. What have I missed (or gained) by leaving one perfectly good painting approach for another?

I guess I never really gave up the looser, broader style, but just never had time for it once I set my goal to get recognition through shows and awards. That goal, somewhat achieved, had a price. A full sheet now takes me hours or days to complete - the freer style was much faster. Of course, judging by inventory I don't need to produce more paintings! Could the faster painting style have become show/award material? Well, if I had continued with that style for the last 20 years, I would certainly, by now, have some winners. I now see that I could have worked with it forever. It was 10 years before I'd win a serious award, and that was with a gouache resist technique.

The fact is, I'm happy with my painting career at this point, more with the teaching than the production, but still happy. I still struggle in the studio, in the galleries, and in the classroom. However, this article shouldn't be so much about me but about what *you* can get out of it, which is mostly up to you. But, before you undertake a sea-change in your work, maybe you can get some advice from others whose word you trust. Maybe you can ask yourself some questions: What other aspects of my work will suffer from a change in approach and style? How will this benefit me *overall* in the coming years? Does what I have to say in this medium work best with my current approach? If so, do I just need to figure out more about how to focus and tweak rather than change my whole painting style?

You could benefit from some insightful pondering. Because you might change anyhow.

Quotes Quotas

Quotes are all the rage these days among watercolor teachers and writers. Frank Webb has hundreds - makes you wonder how they all have time to paint.

But lo and behold, when I was in the Norton Museum of Art in West Palm Beach, FL awhile back, I walked into a small circular lobby where, enshrined in plaques on the walls, in frosted glass, were quotes from no less than ten or so artists, none active before 1850. A few bore thoughts worth some study, and maybe some comparison of ideas. A few were pretty obvious. But all were interesting, since they gave some insight into what the artists themselves thought art was.

"What is art?" is a subject most often argued by philosophers, but more practically, used by the people who actually do the art. And, of course, that means there's a wide range of ideas afloat about art and its definition. So, I'm sure there are many late night discussions about the theory, philosophy, and meaning of art. But I don't do that. I just assume that what I make in my studio is art, and so it is!

What do you think art is? Do you need to think about it? Does a musician really need to think about those things when playing a beautiful piece of Mozart or Bach (two of my faves, anyhow). But there is a more important issue here – do you think of yourself as an artist? If so, what kind of artist? Are you an impressionist, a modernist, a realist or any other kind of "ist"? Whose art do you like? Cezanne, Rembrandt, Michelangelo, Edward Hopper, cave paintings? And how do these artists come through in your paintings? Do you copy their styles, do you live their kind of lives (a very dangerous thing in many cases)? Do you wish you were living in the Renaissance, early Egypt, or maybe classical Greece?

Well, maybe it's something you need to think about. When I read about artists' lives and their responses to other artists' work and lives, I'm often surprised at what they say.

Richard Diebenkorn, the wonderful California abstractionist, was known to be a big fan of Edward Hopper's works, but no one knew why. Finally a friend as well as critic at the Whitney retrospective of Diebenkorn's work asked him what he liked about Hopper. Diebenkorn responded, "The diagonals". When I read this I thought he was kidding, until I started looking at work by both artists. Their work couldn't be more different in content, but Diebenkorn's "Ocean Park" series (painted over a 25 year period) features very geometric compositions, with occasional subtle often shallow diagonals. Hopper favored early or late light so the rays are slanted very little, using the same diagonals in his shadow work.

The great ones are *always* aware of what they look at and what they see in their heroes' works. What do you like best about your painting? Doing it or planning it? Painting alone or as a social event? And what do you like about others' paintings? About museum paintings? When you say, "I like that!" what do you like about it?

Where I'm going with this is that I think it's great to set up and paint every day or week or whatever, but if you are more aware of your own likes, biases, or even out and out dislikes in art, you'll be better able to focus on what you *do* like and how to paint it. The more you paint what you like, the more you'll like your paintings, and the more you'll want to paint them better and better. And eventually you'll say, "I love my paintings, and can't wait to see them on a wall!"

Now, wouldn't that make a nice quote?

Accentuate the Positive

You might be familiar with Johnny Mercer's great hit song with the above title. On the recording, the song was presented as sermon for a congregation, and the full message is: "accentuate the positive; eliminate the negative; latch on to the affirmative - don't mess with Mr. In-Between!" There's much to be said for this little ditty, released in 1944, the same year as the Normandy Invasion. I'm sure it gave some hope to lots of those who wanted to see their loved ones come home from World War II.

Quoting this song is a reminder that the message can be applied to any number of situations, endeavors or attitudes; even painting. We all suffer from some self-recrimination at times ..."Wow is this BAD!" or "I'll NEVER be able to do this right". The fact is we can make it good, and we can learn to do things right. It's my belief we can all create art worthy of praise for its interest, content, and context, and we can all come to recognize those abilities in ourselves.

How? By a change in attitude toward your work. More and more it seems that my primary duty to students as a teacher is getting them to believe in themselves as artists.

I teach in a very traditional way: with lecture, assignment, and critique. Whatever the students have done as an assignment is given the fairest evaluation I can give, especially in consideration of the objectives of the assignment. One way I like to do this is to say, "Name three things you like about this and three things you don't." Answers are random, especially with those new to my methods, but almost always new students start with what they DON'T LIKE and can't see anything they DO LIKE. Then it's up to me to point out what I LIKE and what could be improved. Their work is often *much better* than they can see because they invariably compare it to the work experienced artists produce.

Now, in all fairness, how can a beginner expect to paint as well as an advanced, studied artist? Why should there be any comparison or embarrassment? Maybe because we forget that learning takes time and dedication and more time. It also involves clear goals and finding ways to achieve what you want to achieve.

Here are some methods I've found helpful for me to learn:

-Clarify and simplify what you *need* to know (ask a teacher or a more advanced fellow artist for help if needed). If the project is complex it's still often made up of simple parts. Once you've identified the parts, try to find answers in books, online or other ready sources, then practice improving only those parts until you've got them down. Only then try them in a painting.

-If you like a painting by an artist you know, ask them to explain the progression of it; what was first, what was second, etc. and why. You'll find different artists work differently for the most part, but specific materials, in this case watercolors, work much the same for everyone because they usually require a certain sequencing of application and technique.

-Be patient with yourself. Know that you can learn over time. You can set time goals if you want, but art seems to sink into different minds at different rates. You might not understand value as quickly as your pal, but you might have it all over her with color!

-Always take time in your painting to ask yourself what you *like* about your work. Is it the feel? The color? The design? The trees? The negative spaces? The doing of it? You need to know what you like best because then you'll feel better about your work as a whole and can concentrate on bringing the rest of it up to that same level of enjoyment.

Accomplished artists know what they like and you should know what you like. It might take starters a while to figure this out, but what you "like" is usually what you do best. When you know what you do best, and you like it, you can use it, even exploit it, to make the painting your own. If you don't believe it, think about artists you know who do that; how about Carol Frye and her stick figures? Susan Webb Tregay and her gawky girls on bikes? Frank Webb and his semi-realistic boat docks? Janet Rogers and her effortless florals? The list goes on.

I don't think these are tricks to make their art stand out. I believe these VERY talented artists are painting what they know and what they *love*. And I think this is why they're so good at it.

So if you want to be good at something accentuate the positive. Try to find what you really love about it and let everything else follow. You'll find that your list keeps growing, so that when someone asks you to name three things you like about your painting, your only response will be, "Which three?"

Getting to Know Your Painting

I'm not used to talking about my work - at least not the gouache resist big female nudes I've been doing for over 20 years now. Showing as a group, I thought they looked great alongside Marianna Ross's soaring, gracefully colorful painted silks. But then I had to talk about them in a "gallery talk" - not easy for me because I didn't know where these paintings came from or where they're going exactly.

In fact I was examining a segment of my art that I feel is my best work. They win awards, get in shows, bring praise (for instance, one student called them "great big women in weird colors"), but I never had dealt with where they came from or where they were headed in a concerted, clear analytical way. So, I bravely went where I had never gone before. How?

Right or wrong, I started with what I knew. I love color, and surface interest, which the resist technique offers, and which are strong in all my paintings. I love design, using the figures as central design shapes. And I love expressive figures, using distortion, color, design and other means to convey the feeling of the picture.

Why monumental nudes? Why always indoors, in some old house with garish wallpaper and lots of pillows? Why before a window with no blinds or curtains? Why the cats? As I looked, the paintings offered some answers:

-These women seem vulnerable because they are unclothed - tension!

-The windows simply amplify that vulnerability - anyone might look in on them at any time. Scary!

-These women are feminine as well as strong and big. Positives!

-These women, whether they like their bodies or not (they may not show up on "America's Next Top Model") still focus on clothing - definitely not guy stuff!

-The houses? The answer to that is I spent 45 years as an architect, and old habits die hard. I just don't know when to stop designing buildings, and I like old ones. I live in an old one now. The pillows and wallpaper are just pattern opportunities - pure fun!

-But the cats? Well, I just *love* the shape of a cat!

In fact, this exercise made me feel pretty good about what I've been doing for all that time. Maybe it's Freudian or maybe it isn't. But I've got my opinions, and you can't beat that when you need to talk about your work. Try it! It may be time to get to know it!

Art Is A Verb

My daughter, Elizabeth King Gerlach, an outstanding author on children's disability issues, once wrote a magazine article which was entitled, "Re*tard* Is A Verb". Somehow I think we should also concentrate on "art" as a verb and not as a noun. Ok, so I'm stretching the simile here, but there is method in this madness. To prove my point, here are three great quotes from Polly Hammett;

"Art is the process not the product..."
The making of art is the important part, not what you hang on the wall. If you sought a specific goal, say to make a perfect copy of a single Wyeth picture, and achieved that goal at age 22, why would you continue with art? Artists like Leonardo, Monet, Picasso and Matisse continued until their passing with creative and fresh concepts, refining what they had discovered through their many years as active and prolific painters.

"Art is experimenting ... not formula ..."
No, Virginia, there is no formula. For if there is an art formula, art is predictable. Everyone agrees (if they know anything at all about art) that it is NOT predictable and should not be so. Formula produces those tatty, foo foo paintings that belong over sofas (do the colors match?). Formula did not produce Polly's work, or Miles Batts' work, or that of a thousand others less gifted, but still working through it all. Finally;

"Art is a search... not an answer..."
Note, she didn't say "struggle" or "question" or "bad paycheck". Art is seeking, looking for answers. If you find *the* answer, you can check in at the bone hotel, because you won't have anything left to live for. But if you find *an* answer which leads to another question, you're making art! Or should I say, "Now you are *arting*"?

Note: The above quotes from Polly Hammett, are used without any permission of hers whatsoever.

That Certain Something

My classes recently asked for some guidance on "loosening up", which I made into a series of exercises (mostly designed to get them out of their comfort zones). I think it helped, and they were happy either with the results or because they didn't have to do any more of those exercises.

My wife, Jane, asked me what I was teaching and I told her "How to loosen up". To which she said, "Why?" I tried to explain that, in spite of the many hard-edged, realistic paintings we see nowadays, there's always an appreciation of watercolor done in a loose, but artistic manner. But that wasn't a good answer, at least for me. Her question focused me on finding out why we like "looseness" in any medium (it seems especially appropriate in watercolor).

I went to my source for information on how and why we got to where we are in art today, *Art and Illusion* by E. H. Gombrich, where I found an answer, or at least a good theory as to why we love "loose". Gombrich investigates how and why we see and comprehend art based on history and visual/cultural norms. He gives insight into the "loose" issue through a comparison of similar works by different Renaissance artists. What he shows is that while the subject, medium, even the composition might be the same, the end product shows one as "looser" than the other, and, in its way, more attractive. Gombrich describes this less specific approach as *"sprezzatura"*, from the Renaissance Italian, which is translated as the ability to perform a difficult act and make it appear easy and natural – a sort of nonchalance. What I call "that certain something".

'Ok,' I said, 'I get that.' John Singer Sargent has been accused by critics as painting only to show his virtuosity, aka, showing off. I figure, who cares? Heck, if I could paint that way I'd "virtuose" all the time too. He had *sprezzatura*!

But on to the crux of the issue! Why would we like rough (loose) over smooth (finished)? One would think the beginning watercolor artist would produce rough work, but I find that (with the exception of children) the more they learn control of the medium, the more detailed they get with their painting, even to the point of confusing the viewer, and seeing their work as amateurish. Logic would say this looseness business is backward thinking; the less detail the better? Crazy talk!

Let's go deeper.

In paintings, if we see every blade of grass, every leaf on the tree, every brick in the wall, etc., we are told exactly, in infinite detail, what the painting is about – the artist's ability to represent what is seen in the real world. But, since we know what grass and trees and bricks look like, we don't get engrossed in the message. It's like reading a book that is a repetition of the alphabet over and over. We get bored. But if we artists can make one stroke of the brush look like a shadow over a field of grass, or make tree foliage become shapes and clusters of leaves in sunlight or shade, we leave something for the viewer to decipher. If we can make that brick wall a statement of shape and color in the overall work with only a few brick-like strokes, it becomes more than a copy of the real world – it's something that involves the viewer in the artist's world. That involvement is what makes us delight in the easy, loose brushwork of so many advanced artists. When we have to decipher that stroke, we take some ownership of the information in the painting.

Not to be didactic, but if we look at history, we'll see that an astounding revolution in painting came when the camera made realism a secondary requirement for painting. The Impressionists moved from expert strokes to dabs of color. The Fauves moved to spots of color exclusive of local color or value. The Expressionists moved to distortion and ambiguity of depth, color, and realism. The Modernists moved to geometric shapes and personal expression on the paper or canvas. And so on to the current day.

The reasons are straightforward: We paint works to be viewed. Those viewing need to be involved. Some like all the bricks. Some like the meaningful brushwork. Some like the breakdown of color and shape up close, but love seeing them melded at a distance. And on and on.

It's ok to paint all the bricks and leaves, but we *really* need to know how to involve ALL viewers in our paintings, not just the brick and leaf lovers. So, keep learning about design, and keep studying other painters' work, and keep asking questions. Keep asking, "How does this painting involve me?" and, when it fits, begin to apply those answers to your own work.

It's not easy, but if you do, people will soon be saying, "Now that's what I call *sprezzatura*!" Or maybe, "This painting has that certain something!"

How To Be A Pro

We are all products of our time, our upbringing and our experience. So is art. We see in art what we know about, accept as normal, and have experience with. But if our grandparents convinced our parents, and they convinced us that art was a waste of time, we'll have that same opinion. If we were taught that the value of art was in its ability to picture things realistically, we're likely to believe the same. And if their standard for quality of art was its degree of realism, we'll think the same. We can't help it.

But the history of art is the history of challenge, of change, and of leading. It is not for the faint of heart or for the copyist. It is the realm of the creative people in the culture of our times.

That great blunderbuss of a teacher, Ed Whitney said people asked him why he was an artist and he responded, "Because it is an honorable profession which produces works of beauty". When I heard this at one of his demos, I was astounded because I'd never thought of art as a "profession" - a kind of work, or a pleasant pastime maybe, but never a profession. Lawyers and doctors have professions, but art? I, the son of an artist, was a product of that same society that portrays artists as goofy outsiders who delight in confounding the public with their suspect activities and the strange work they produce which they (ha-ha) call art.

To be a lawyer or doctor or architect, a license is required, but not to be an artist. Chefs, builders, even gamblers are labeled as "professionals", so I should have been prepared for Whitney's description of an artist. And ever since, I've taken it to heart that to be an artist is to take a place in that long line of professionals who have shaped our view of society as much as society has shaped theirs.

I guess this ramble is about how hard it is to focus on making painting about what's on the paper instead of what's in front of you, and why I try to be forgiving and understanding if people don't get it right away or at all. There was a time when I didn't understand that either, and artists were goofy outsiders calling strange things art. Learning to move toward the painting and away from "the subject" seems counterproductive, but only as long as you're in the copyist zone. When you learn that you are in charge of the work and not the reverse, you are forever absolved from having to reproduce what you see before you. You are no longer judged by verisimilitude. You are on your own. You are an artist.

How can you make it easier when you are the artist – when it really is just up to you and when you have to be held accountable for what you paint? Well here's what works for me:

-Learn the mantra: "This is only paint on paper." Learn to say it early and say it often. If the painting doesn't work, start over.

-Create with elements, judge with principles. Learn the elements of design and how to use them in your work. As you work, think about the principles of design and how your painting is stacking up on that end. Is it balanced? Is there repetition? Is there unity, dominance, contrast? And so on until you know which way you're headed and what's primary in your design.

-Trust yourself. After a lot of time and experience you're going to find that your instincts are carrying you through. The direct line from your brain to the brush tip is simply an express route to making art. The faster you can get the idea there, the better your work will be.

-Find what you love/like in art. Be it flowers, plein air, abstract, portraits, or whatever, it will be better art if you love painting it.

-Try new things. We all get bored with repetition. New stuff from workshops, classes, painting with buddies, new ideas, techniques, whatever, can brighten up your paintings and renew your interest in the medium.

-Find a place and a time to paint regularly. This is hard to do when you have a family, a house, a job, but some regularity can identify that time as "yours". When it's yours, you can do better work and work better.

-When you do something right, say what it was out loud and *listen to remember!* We forget if we don't verbalize.

And again:
- Say the mantra, "This is only paint on paper!"

These are only a few of the tools we can use to progress in our pursuit of better art. So throw off that yoke of social opinion of artists as dorks and turn professional. As my dear mother-in-law used to say, "If you don't think well of yourself, nobody else will!"

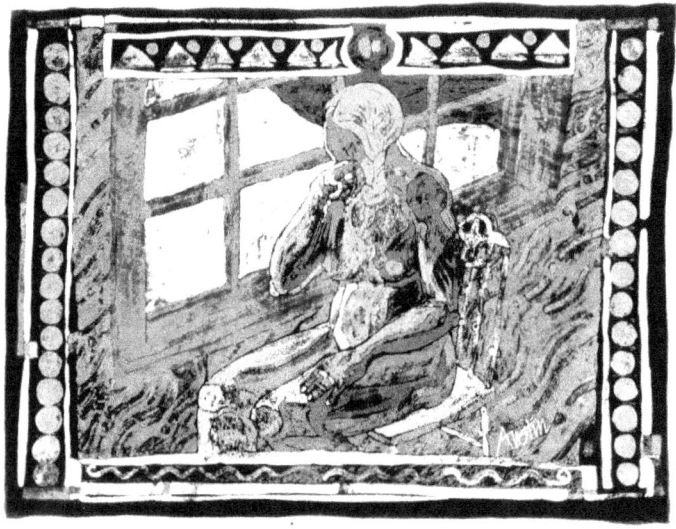

By the Window

ABOUT THE AUTHOR

Ken Austin, NWS, has lived in Orlando, FL for over 25 years. Before moving to Orlando, Ken was president of the Watercolor Art Society - Houston, TX, and served on the Board of Directors there for over six years. Over the past 15 years, Ken has taught lessons and presented demos, lectures, and workshops privately, and he has also taught classes at the community college level.

Ken founded the Central Florida Watercolor Society in 1996, which has grown to a membership of around 200. He is a signature member of the National Watercolor Society and the Florida Watercolor Society, and a member of the Florida Artists Group (FLAG).

Ken was, for ten years, a gallery artist with the Albertson-Peterson Gallery of Winter Park, FL, and for five years was represented by galleries in Clearwater, Jacksonville, as well as Orlando, Florida, where he was a resident studio artist. His teaching experience is broad, including stints with the University of Houston, Texas Southern University, Seminole Community College, and Crealdé School of Art in Winter Park, Florida. Learn more at www.kenaustinartist.com.

www.ingramcontent.com/pod-product-compliance
Lightning Source LLC
Chambersburg PA
CBHW052311220526
45472CB00001B/71